MURDER
AND THE
MEDIA

MURDER AND THE MEDIA

BEHIND THE SCENES OF FOUR HIGH PROFILE MURDERS

ALLISON HOPE WEINER

A POST HILL PRESS BOOK
ISBN: 979-8-89565-134-6
ISBN (eBook): 979-8-89565-135-3

Murder and the Media:
Behind the Scenes of Four High Profile Murders

Cover design by Cody Corcoran

All people, locations, events, and situations are portrayed to the best of the author's memory. While all of the events described are true, many names and identifying details have been changed to protect the privacy of the people involved.

Post Hill Press
New York • Nashville
posthillpress.com

Published in the United States of America
1 2 3 4 5 6 7 8 9 10

For Jody, the love of my life and my partner in crime.

CONTENTS

FOREWORD

There are some things no one can really understand unless they were there. And that's how I feel about the night Allison and I went onto a pitch-dark farm in the middle of Oklahoma looking for the exact location where several bodies had been buried. I thought she was nuts, but she pushed us to continue down the dark, dirt road. That's how Allison and I operate together. When I'm nervous, she pushes me and vice versa. She gave the pep talk and I hit the gas past a chain link fence. The owner (who was armed by the way) was not initially happy to see us. And neither was his dog. But Allison talked to him, and an hour later he took us to the spot.

How did this sophisticated Los Angeles lawyer turned journalist so quickly bond with an Oklahoma farmer in the middle of the night? I know, it's hard to believe. But I've seen Allison do it countless times.

There is nothing easy about what Allison Weiner does. The only way to truly get exclusive information on a developing crime story is to fully immerse yourself. And that is what she does every single time. There is no middle ground with Allison—and no sleeping. I realized that when we started working together years ago. There's no phoning it in with Allison, and no giving up. Her fuel is Tootsie Rolls and an unrelenting desire to get to the truth.

Allison has a way of talking her way into places journalists are not allowed. It's because police, witnesses, and victims trust her—and they should. Her integrity guides her in every case. She isn't afraid to take risks—but never at the price of an innocent victim.

Nothing will stop Allison. I remember walking up to a courthouse with Allison to try and get an interview with a sheriff. Reporters had been trying for weeks. There was a big sign taped to the front door said No Interviews. No Media. I was discouraged, but Allison wasn't. A few days later we walked through the door for an exclusive interview with law enforcement. Allison always finds a way to get in.

I think what is most special about the access Allison gets is unlike other reporters—she never sneaks her way in. She's methodical, ethical, and respectful. She's the real deal. And sources know they can trust her. It's why Allison can deliver a crime story unlike any other journalist can.

Brian Entin, News Nation Senior National Correspondent
and host of YouTube's @BrianEntinInvestigates

INTRODUCTION

This book is a compilation of four high-profile murder cases that I've covered during my twenty-five-year career as an investigative journalist. My focus in writing about these specific cases was to give readers a chance to learn new information and details that they couldn't find out about any other way. The stories in this book are ones that I've never written about before in an article or discussed on a newscast or a primetime crime show. I wrote this book to give readers the unique experience of being a real investigative reporter, working behind the scenes, doing day-to-day reporting on a crime by speaking to a bevy of both reputable and disreputable sources—providing the down-and-dirty details of how real investigative journalism happens. In this book, I have written specific details about crimes that are rarely made public—including my conversations with a grieving family before a famous murder trial; interviews with friends of the killer that never made it into a television show about the crime; my chance meeting with one killer in a ladies' bathroom; and a plethora of behind-the-scenes interviews with prosecutors, criminal defense lawyers, jury consultants, and law enforcement, all of whom were working diligently to control the narrative as they advanced their agendas.

I have always had a passion for finding out things that people didn't want me to know—hence my choice of career. Even in the early years when I graduated from law school and began practicing law that dealt mainly with the entertainment industry, I spent a great deal of time researching the facts of any case I handled, sometimes even driving to where a particular event occurred to interview anyone who might have some helpful information. After leaving the practice of law, it seemed a natural progression for me to become an investigative journalist. I began my journalism career as a freelance journalist, covering a criminal case involving a murder that happened in Horn Lake, Mississippi, more than twenty-five years ago. The case involved a woman named Linda Leedom, a local accountant and nurse who murdered her best friend for insurance money. I flew to Mississippi from Los Angeles to interview the members of the law enforcement, fire department, and prosecutors involved in the investigation and prosecution of Leedom, along with the defendant's family, friends, and neighbors. Next, I turned my attention to the victim and her family, ultimately spending weeks in Horn Lake collecting documents, transcripts, and photographs before covering Leedom's trial. I learned during the Leedom case to employ many of the skills that I'd honed as an attorney: to look at the story from every angle and to gather my facts from a multitude of sources, through both formal and informal requests. When covering a trial, one cannot rely solely on what is allowed to be presented in court to understand what happened in the case. That is a story that must be woven together by a thorough and unrestrained investigation of all the supposed facts that both the defense and the prosecution present.

My career started to take off when *Entertainment Weekly* hired me to cover civil legal disputes and crime stories related to the entertainment industry. Not long after I started at the magazine, famed actor Robert Blake's wife, Bonny Lee Bakley, was murdered after having dinner with Blake at a Studio City restaurant. One of my earliest stories for the magazine was about that case, written before Robert Blake was even arrested. I did numerous interviews for the story, including some rather revealing ones with Blake's famed LA attorney, Harland Braun. During my time at *Entertainment Weekly*, I covered notorious Hollywood trials, including the Michael Jackson case in which he was acquitted of charges of sexual molestation, Phil Spector's murder trial, Winona Ryder's shoplifting trial in Beverly Hills, and Robert Downey Jr.'s arrest for drug use and three-year sentence in state prison, of which he served fifteen months.

I left *Entertainment Weekly* to work at the *New York Times,* where I covered the wiretapping and conspiracy case against Anthony Pellicano, which resulted in the conviction of Pellicano and several of his high-profile clients. I also covered the trial for the *Huffington Post*, publishing a series of illegal recordings of various Hollywood celebrities who had hired Pellicano, including Courtney Love and Chris Rock, as well as those who had been victimized by the private detective and his clients, like comedian Garry Shandling. After publishing many of the documents and audio recordings for the *Huffington Post,* several defense attorneys attempted to have the court prevent me from publishing any more "sealed documents or recordings" and to have me held in contempt. They failed. The FBI also launched an investigation to discover my source or sources. They also failed.

After years of writing about murder cases for magazines and newspapers, I transitioned into television. I also hosted my own YouTube channel, Crime Time, for several years, covering the major criminal cases of the day with renowned legal and law enforcement experts and newsmakers. I ultimately opted to end my involvement in the show and went to work for ABC News *20/20*, where I covered some of the biggest crime stories in the country, both present and past. While at ABC, I worked on a multitude of stories, including the Holly Bobo case, which is included in this book. Although *20/20* featured exclusive interviews with Holly Bobo's family shortly after her murder trial, those interviews did not feature much of the information that I wrote about in this book. Much of my work on the story didn't make it into the final piece for a myriad of reasons. While at ABC News *20/20*, I worked with Diane Sawyer and Mark Robertson covering the Turpin case involving thirteen children who were horrifically abused, starved, and held captive by their parents in Perris, California. The story was dubbed "House of Horrors." I also covered the Phil Hartman murder, the Manson Family murders, the Noura Jackson case, Holly Bobo's murder, Harvey Weinstein, and a lengthy list of other high-profile cases. I am currently working as a senior producer for NewsNation, where I have worked on crime stories all over the country, including notorious cases such as the murder of the "Idaho Four" by Bryan Kohberger and the Sean "Puffy" Combs sex-trafficking trial.

Given my lengthy career covering murder cases for both print and television, I am always aware that much of my reporting on a case never becomes a public story. Some things happen before, during, and after a murder trial that don't fit into a linear story for print and, particularly, for television. After years of working on crime stories, I've encountered hundreds of unknown moments. These include conversations with a victim's mother, chats with the first responders, and observations of lawyer interactions during trials, all of which take place in courthouse hallways. These unknown stories are usually the ones that I tell my friends and family about during dinner or at a cocktail party or that I share with younger reporters just starting and looking for advice. My stories are varied, gleaned from years of experience, and often are about dangerous or difficult moments in my career. Sometimes they're about something that happened long before a trial started—drinks with a defense attorney quietly expressing disgust for his client, an investigator who's convinced that his co-workers arrested the wrong suspect, or getting evidence from a witness who discreetly drops a thumb drive into my handbag before a court hearing. These stories often involve secrecy or danger, with me driving miles to meet a witness in a private location, hoping to garner information that has yet to be published.

Many of my best behind-the-scenes stories are included in the cases that I've covered here. The book is divided into four sections, each focusing on a different trial. Within each section, there are three chapters that lay out the details of the case. The first chapter covers the actual crime case and the key players. For example, in the first chapter, I cover the murder of Holly Bobo, a twenty-year-old nursing student who was kidnapped from her own remote Tennessee home and then raped and murdered. The second chapter of each section, which includes a great deal of never-revealed information about the murder case, covers the investigation, the media coverage, and includes most of the significant interviews that I conducted while covering the case. The third chapter of each section details how the trial ended, any appeals or other events that happened posttrial, as well as setting forth the current status of the case.

When you have finished this book, you will have an understanding of the following from someone who has been there:

1. How do the mainstream media and the alternative media cover a criminal trial?
2. How did I manage to get a victim's family to speak to me? How do I convince anyone involved in a criminal case to speak with me?
3. How do I find witnesses or individuals with knowledge of a criminal case when I don't have any obvious way to contact them?
4. Which people are most likely to provide me with information about the investigation during a criminal trial? Law enforcement, lawyers, prosecutors, or maybe witnesses?
5. What does it feel like to be a family member of a victim in a high-profile murder case? What does it feel like to be in the middle of a media storm?
6. What is the dialogue that happens informally between the prosecution and the defense attorneys prior to, during, and after a trial? Are the dust-ups between attorneys and prosecutors in court merely performative? How do I find out what was discussed at sidebars?
7. How do the police investigation and/or interviews influence the prosecutor's decision on the charges that are brought against the defendant?

8. What is it like to be a family member of a notorious defendant charged with murder?
9. What are the roles of various private investigators, mediums, talking heads, and other ancillary figures in a notorious murder trial? Who ultimately profits?

When you finish this book, you will know how the criminal legal process works for all of the parties involved in a criminal trial.

CHAPTER ONE

Tennessee Rose: The Murder of Holly Bobo

The case of Holly Bobo gripped me long before I ever set foot in the courtroom. In 2011 Holly—a twenty-year-old nursing student—was abducted from her home in rural Tennessee, then raped and murdered. For three agonizing years, despite tireless efforts by law enforcement and her family, there were no answers. Her remains weren't discovered until 2014. The case didn't go to trial until 2017, seven years after Holly's abduction and murder. By the time I attended the proceedings in 2017, many details surrounding the investigation and prosecution had never been made public. But through months of reporting, I uncovered key information that revealed what really happened behind the scenes—how the investigation unfolded, where it faltered, and who was ultimately brought to justice. I remained objective throughout. But even now, the horror of what happened to Holly Bobo lingers with me.

All murder stories are hard to cover. But Holly Bobo's case was especially difficult—both heartless and haunting in ways I still struggle to comprehend. Holly was twenty years old, beloved by her family and friends, and driven by a passion for nursing. She was dating a kind young man, studying hard for a future she was building piece by piece. Her life was unfolding exactly as it should have—until the morning of April 13, 2011, when everything fell apart. As the prosecutor, Paul Haggerman, would later tell the jury in his opening statement at the trial of Holly's killer, she grew up in the ranch-style home that her father, Dana, built with his father. It was just outside of Parsons, Tennessee, in Decatur County. It was where they were supposed to be safe. It was their home. Dana and his wife, Karen, moved into the home in 1982, which was nestled on twenty-three wooded acres at the end of Swan Johnson Road in Darden, Tennessee. It was the kind of rural place where the gravel crunches under your tires long before you reach the house. The town had fewer than four hundred residents in 2011, and Nashville—the nearest city—was more than a hundred miles away. Darden is now home to an estimated 612 people.[1,2]

Holly's childhood was shaped by the outdoors. She and her older brother, Clint, spent countless hours exploring the woods, riding ATVs, and swimming in nearby lakes. She loved horses. She loved her home. And the home itself was peaceful,

---

1 "Holly Bobo Murder Trial Prosecution Opening Statements." YouTube, Law&Crime Network, 11 Sept. 2017, www.youtube.com/watch?v=tVnbHMFjPSo&list=PLoW1SIeAWaWbNG-RXiqJeKy2ZWK_JTlb4&index=2.,

2 "Holly Bobo Murder Trial Defense Opening Statements." YouTube, Law&Crime Network, 11 Sept. 2017, https://www.youtube.com/watch?v=PMbL_6OBEgY&list=PLoW1SIeAWaWbNG-RXiqJeKy2ZWK_JTlb4&index=3.

surrounded by forest, set apart from view, and far removed from anything resembling danger. Dana Bobo ran a tree-service business. His wife, Karen, taught second grade. They'd been married for twenty-nine years, building a loving, tight-knit family where both children thrived. After high school, Holly enrolled in a nursing bridge program at UT Martin Parsons Center, just four miles from home. She and Clint still lived with their parents, sharing meals, laughter, and long conversations around the kitchen table.

On school days, the Bobo house stirred early. Dana left first—out the door by 5:30 a.m. for work. Clint usually followed around 6:00 a.m., heading to UT Martin to study social work. Karen would generally head out by 7:00 a.m. for her teaching job. Holly's schedule varied, but on the morning of April 13, she got up around 4:00 a.m. to study for a nursing exam. Dana didn't see her before he left, but he noticed the light under her door and asked if she needed gas money. She said yes, and he left a twenty-dollar bill on the counter and told her he loved her. Karen, already awake, shut Clint's door—his TV was too loud—then peeked in on Holly, who was sitting on her bed with a book in her lap. They chatted briefly, and Karen made her daughter lunch, slipping Dana's twenty into Holly's purse. After showering and dressing, Karen came out to find Holly now at the dining table, still studying. Holly asked for muffins. Karen placed some in the microwave and told her how to warm them up. At around 7:00 a.m., she hugged her daughter, said "I love you," and headed out the door. She didn't know it would be the last time she'd ever see Holly alive.

Roughly forty minutes later, a neighbor heading to work heard a woman screaming, "Stop! Stop it!" He thought it was just an argument between family members. But then the scream cut off sharply, and the dogs began barking wildly. He paused, looked around, and eventually drove off—still uneasy. From his truck, he called his mother and asked her to check in on the Bobos. She called Karen at the school, leaving a message with the front office.

Back on Swan Johnson Road, Clint Bobo had overslept. He woke to the dog barking and drifted back to sleep, but the barking continued and woke him again. Curious, he looked out the window and saw that Holly's car was still in the driveway, which struck him as odd, as she should've been at school already. He left a voicemail for his mom, asking if Holly was home. Karen, who'd just received a message from the neighbor, immediately called Clint back. She told him Holly should have been in class. "Go find her," she said, her voice rising. Then she hung up and dialed 911, but she reached the wrong county dispatcher. It would be the first of several critical delays.

Clint moved to a window overlooking the carport and noticed Holly's car was still there. He heard voices—one male, one female—and raised the blinds. He could see two people kneeling, but not their faces. He recognized Holly's voice. The man's voice sounded agitated. He assumed it was her boyfriend, Drew, and figured they were arguing. Still uneasy, Clint called both of their phones. No answer. Karen called back. When Clint told her he'd seen Holly walking into the woods with a man in camouflage, she screamed, "That's not Drew!" Drew, she explained, was miles away on his grandmother's land, turkey hunting. "Get a gun," she said. "Shoot him!" Still thinking it might be Drew, Clint hesitated. But he grabbed his revolver and stepped outside. That's when he noticed a pool of blood near

Holly's car. He followed the trail toward the woods, stopping at the tree line, listening. Then a neighbor, Cathy, pulled into the driveway. She'd heard the scream too. Now alarmed, Clint called 911. It was 8:10 a.m. when the first Decatur County deputy arrived.[3]

Meanwhile, Dana Bobo received a call at work: "Holly's been taken." He rushed home, grabbed his pistol, and joined the swelling crowd gathering on the property. Within hours, state and federal authorities arrived—the TBI, FBI, US Marshals, even a SWAT team. A helicopter circled overhead. Searchers fanned out across the twenty-eight acres, looking for any sign of Holly. In the chaos, Dana realized that no one had secured the crime scene. Neighbors and searchers were trampling through the carport where blood was still visible. Desperate to preserve what little evidence remained, he pulled out two lawn chairs and strung pink tape across the garage. Only later that morning would police arrive with the yellow tape.

The Suspects

The first law enforcement officer to respond that April morning was Deputy Tony Weber of the Decatur County Sheriff's Office. After hearing a report from 911 dispatch that a young woman had been taken into the woods, Weber raced to the Bobo residence with lights and sirens. When he arrived, he found Clint Bobo standing outside with a neighbor, Cathy Wise.

At first, Weber wasn't convinced that a crime had occurred. Despite the dispatcher's report that Holly Bobo had been taken

[3] "Timeline of Holly Bobo Case," *The Tennessean*. September 9, 2014.

against her will, he seemed uncertain. He began asking Clint questions that reflected doubt: Was it possible Holly had gone to school early? Could she have willingly walked into the woods? Was the man with her her boyfriend—or maybe a cousin?

Clint stood by what he'd seen. He told Weber that Holly had walked into the woods with a man in camouflage and that it wasn't her boyfriend, Drew. The man was bulkier, with dark hair spilling over his collar. Clint briefly considered whether it might have been their cousin Richie, who had a similar build. But what struck Clint most was the tension in their voices. He was adamant: Holly had not gone willingly.

Even so, Weber remained dubious—until Clint pointed out the pool of blood next to Holly's car. Only then did the gravity of the situation begin to register.

Weber asked Clint to write down everything he could remember and began taping off the scene. Moments later, Karen Bobo arrived. Overcome with panic, she jumped from her car and sprinted into the woods, screaming her daughter's name. Weber chased after her, trying to restrain her. Through her panic, Karen managed to tell him that Holly still had her cell phone. That single detail might have made a difference—if the next steps had been handled more effectively.

Weber quickly called dispatch to initiate a phone trace. But technical red tape bogged down the process. AT&T required a supervisor's signature before releasing location data. Weber faxed the necessary forms but made a crucial mistake: he requested cell tower "pings" every fifteen minutes, unaware that updates could have been provided every sixty seconds. When the ping data finally came through, it was emailed to his department inbox—delayed, and too imprecise to track Holly in real time. Worse still, Weber didn't know how to interpret the GPS coordinates. He passed the data along to other agencies, but critical time had already been lost.

For the Bobo family, that first hour became a source of lasting grief. The deputy hadn't treated the situation without any urgency. No roadblocks were set up. No immediate perimeter was established. And Holly's phone, which could have been used to triangulate her location, wasn't tracked in real time. The first agent from the TBI to arrive at the Bobo home, Brent Booth, would later testify at trial that law enforcement got pings from Holly's phone that could have helped locate her while she was still alive. However, experts noted that the phones in 2011 could locate a person in a general area, but not with the specificity they could in 2017. Investigators would testify at the trial in 2017 that the final pings on Holly's phone came from the Yellow Springs area, where Holly Bobo's remains were ultimately found three years later. According to investigators at trial, the first ping came in at 8:56 a.m., but by 9:06 a.m., Holly's phone was dead. Investigator Booth admitted during his trial testimony, "We made mistakes that I will take with me for the rest of my life."

When agents from the Tennessee Bureau of Investigation first arrived at the Bobo home, they focused not outward—but inward. From the beginning, they viewed Clint Bobo with suspicion. They questioned why he hadn't run after his sister immediately. Why hadn't he called 911 right away? Why did he wait after hearing raised voices? Their skepticism hardened quickly. Some agents believed Clint was lying. Others suspected drugs played a role—that Holly's abduction was connected to a deal gone wrong involving her brother. Rumors swirled that Clint was hiding something.

He wasn't. Clint cooperated fully with law enforcement and repeatedly told them everything he could remember. But for days, even as the window to find Holly narrowed, the TBI remained fixated on him. Dana Bobo eventually pulled aside one of the FBI agents and said what many in the family were thinking: "If you think we're involved, then keep some agents here. But get the others the hell out there to find Holly."

The investigation eventually widened. Officers canvassed the area, questioning neighbors about anything unusual they may have seen or heard. One of those neighbors was John Babb, a retired rear admiral in the U.S. Public Health Service who owned 150 wooded acres bordering the Bobos' land. He'd known the family for years—Holly often rode her horse on his trails, and Dana had done tree work for him.

On the morning Holly disappeared, Babb and a friend were preparing to go fishing near a lake on his property. Around 7:30 a.m., Babb was standing at the levee when he heard a sound—something sharp and distressing, like cats fighting or a high-pitched screech. He looked toward Swan Johnson Road but saw nothing. Then he heard the roar of an engine.

A white pickup truck flew past—faster than he'd ever seen a vehicle go on that gravel road, probably fifty or sixty miles per hour. It had an extended cab and was racing south, just beyond the edge of the Bobo property. He turned to his friend and said what they were both thinking: "That truck was flying."

It was another clue. But like so much in this case, it would take time—too much time—before anyone connected it to the men who'd taken Holly Bobo.

The Search

The months that followed Holly Bobo's disappearance were a living hell for her family. Life as they knew it came to a halt. From sunrise to sunset, they joined neighbors, friends, and hundreds of volunteers in a desperate search—combing woods, scouring roadsides, checking abandoned buildings, sheds, barns, and lakes. Dana Bobo didn't return to work for eight weeks. Every day, he searched.

The family left no stone unturned. They looked through vacant and occupied homes, traveled miles beyond the location of Holly's last cell phone ping, and followed any lead, no matter how remote. FBI agents were present in the early days but soon departed. The responsibility of fielding tips—some credible, many cruel—fell on the Bobos themselves.

The family turned to the media for help. Karen gave out her personal cell phone number, pleading with the public for any information. While many responded with support, others exploited the tragedy for attention or money. Online, the cruelty was relentless. Some accused the Bobos of being negligent parents. Others claimed the kidnapping was a hoax. The most vicious attacks targeted Clint—calling him a coward, a drug addict, even a sexual deviant for not intervening the morning Holly was taken.

Still, the family pressed on. They spoke to anyone who might offer insight: law enforcement, private investigators, psychics, and self-proclaimed mediums. Karen followed up on every call, no matter how implausible. Sightings came in from as far as California and New York. At night, she prayed and filled her journal with desperate pleas to God for Holly's return.

Clint withdrew. The guilt and shame, coupled with the relentless suspicion and internet harassment, took a heavy toll. Dana remained determined. He searched every day, trudging through rough terrain, clinging to hope that Holly was alive, being held somewhere, waiting for rescue. At night, he dreamed of her calling out for him. Law enforcement continued to investigate other leads, but many agents remained fixated on Clint. Some were convinced he was hiding something. They questioned why he hadn't chased after Holly or called 911 sooner.

TBI agent Terry Britt, who was the lead investigator on the scene following the abduction, told me in the months before the trial, that Clint Bobo was the TBI's main suspect for years and they were convinced he wasn't telling them the truth.

"There was an agent that told him [Clint Bobo] during an interrogation, 'Somebody right now is raping your sister because you're sitting here lying to us. We are lucky he didn't kill himself after everything that took place,' Dicus said. 'I think the Bobo family are the best people in the world.'"

Dicus believed Clint was telling the truth after interviewing him. While other agents pushed to wiretap Clint's phone, Dicus pursued a different suspect: Terry Britt, a known sex offender.

Britt claimed he was shopping for a bathtub at the time of Holly's disappearance and provided receipts to support his alibi. Dicus suspected the receipts were obtained by Britt's wife to cover for him. He believed Britt had abducted Holly, sexually assaulted her, and likely killed her.

Despite pressure from him to focus on Clint, Dicus persisted in investigating Terry Britt. Karen Bobo told me that "Terry Dicus knew we were innocent. He thought it might be Terry Britt who took Holly, but I never felt like it was Terry Britt. I talked to Jan, Terry Britt's wife—I don't think it was him. Terry's modus operandi didn't fit with Holly. He always picked out people that he knew—girls that were prostitutes. Holly had never been anywhere he'd been."

Agent Dicus, however, remained dogged in his attempt to find evidence against Britt. He obtained voice samples from Britt and asked Clint if he recognized the voice from that morning. Clint narrowed it down to two—one of them was Britt. The other belonged to a random felon. Dicus later showed Clint a photo lineup that included Britt. Again, Clint couldn't make a definitive identification.

Frustrated by the continued suspicion from the TBI, Karen and Dana sought legal advice. A friend referred them to Steve Farese Sr., a high-profile criminal defense attorney. Farese had recently gained national attention for successfully defending Mary Winkler, a preacher's wife who shot her abusive husband. Now, he agreed to represent Clint and assist the family in dealing with the mounting pressure. Farese believed in Clint's innocence, and he was alarmed by the toll repeated interrogations had taken on Clint's mental health. To help clear his name, Clint agreed to take a polygraph, with Farese by his side. He passed. Still, investigators dismissed the results and demanded another test. Even after other suspects were arrested in connection with Holly's disappearance, the rumors about Clint persisted. Online speculation was unrelenting. For Clint Bobo, the psychological damage was lasting—and profound.

The Remains

Three years after Holly Bobo vanished, her family finally got the confirmation they had both prayed for and dreaded. On September 7, 2014, two men searching for ginseng in the woods came across a bucket filled with human remains. The discovery was made not far from Holly's home. Within twenty-four hours, authorities confirmed what many had feared: the remains were Holly's. She had died from a single gunshot wound to the back of her head. The heartbreaking recovery of her remains brought no immediate clarity. Investigators still had no definitive answers about who had killed her—or why. With the case now formally a homicide, the Tennessee Bureau of Investigation revisited earlier suspects: Zach and Dylan Adams, brothers from nearby Holladay; their friend Shayne Austin; and Austin's cousin, Jason Autry. The four men were known to be close—and known to law enforcement. All struggled with serious drug addiction. All had criminal records.

Karen Bobo had urged police to question them in the days after Holly disappeared. She'd heard the names early on and flagged them for investigators. But at the time, the local sheriff dismissed the lead outright. He told her there was "no way" any of those men were involved.

That changed after Dylan Adams, who was serving time for an unrelated crime, was interrogated about Holly's disappearance. During that session, Dylan allegedly confessed to raping Holly and implicated Zach, Autry, and Austin in the kidnapping, rape, and murder. His statement led the TBI to obtain a search warrant for Zach Adams's home. On March 5, 2014, Zach was indicted for aggravated kidnapping and felony first-degree murder. Jason Autry was indicted the following month, with both men later facing additional charges for rape. Dylan Adams, too, was charged.

Shayne Austin initially cooperated. He agreed to a deal with prosecutors in exchange for information. But investigators later claimed he violated the agreement by refusing to tell the full truth. Before he could be arrested, Austin was found dead in Florida—an apparent suicide. Authorities concluded his death was a further indication of his involvement.

All four men—Zach and Dylan Adams, Shayne Austin, and Jason Autry—lived near Holly's home. The Adams brothers knew her. Austin had been seen in the area. Autry would later claim he didn't even know who Holly Bobo was. But the case against them moved slowly. It wasn't until September 2017—more than six years after Holly disappeared—that the first trial began.

Dylan Adams, who had allegedly confessed on video, was portrayed by his attorney as mentally disabled and unable to fully comprehend the nature of his statements. The defense claimed he had been illegally detained and coerced, and that his limited intellectual ability made him especially vulnerable during interrogation. Zach Adams and Jason Autry, meanwhile, insisted on their innocence. That changed when prosecutors offered Autry a deal in exchange for his testimony. He agreed—and confessed. According to the defense, however, Autry's statements were never turned over in discovery. Despite the implications of his own admitted involvement, Autry was granted immunity by the state for his cooperation. His testimony would become central to the prosecution's case. What remained unclear was whether the confessions—one from a man with cognitive challenges, the other from a man who secured immunity—would hold up under scrutiny in court.

CHAPTER TWO

The Investigation Behind the Scenes

I never assume anything when I'm reporting a story. Even after someone has been arrested or indicted, I try to withhold judgment. In the Bobo case, what I discovered during my investigation raised troubling questions—not only about the defendants' guilt, but also about the police work that led to their arrests. Despite my deep sympathy for Holly's family, I began to wonder if the wrong men had been charged with her kidnapping, rape, and murder. To report honestly, I knew I had to separate my compassion for the Bobos from the facts I was uncovering.

Holly Bobo's trial was scheduled for September 2017. I had already been investigating the case earlier that year, but once I began working with ABC News *20/20*, I intensified my reporting efforts. I wanted to bring the story to the network—but I still hadn't secured an interview with the Bobo family. I'd left messages and sent a note. No response. Eventually, I reached out to their attorney and my friend, Steve Farese Sr.

I first met Steve while covering another Tennessee case: an eighteen-year-old girl convicted of stabbing her mother to death. Though he wasn't involved in that case, I already knew his name from his defense of Mary Winkler. I'd made a point of meeting him in Ashland, Mississippi, after that story wrapped. Over the years, we worked on several stories together and built a real friendship.

Despite his packed trial calendar, Steve agreed to represent the Bobos pro bono. He never said exactly why, but it was clear he understood the depth of the family's grief. With years of experience in high-profile cases, Steve also understood the pressure investigators were under—and how that pressure had unfairly led them toward Clint Bobo. He shielded the family from aggressive media, gave statements at public events, and finally succeeded in getting the TBI to stop badgering Clint. He also kept private investigators and so-called internet sleuths at bay. But there was only so much anyone could do to ease the family's suffering.

When we spoke about my doing a story for *20/20* with executive producer David Sloan and Elizabeth Vargas. Steve encouraged me to look beyond the horror of Holly's murder and focus on what the family had endured in the years since. They had been revictimized, he explained—not just by the public, but by the very people tasked with helping them. Holly was missing for three years, during which time the family was bombarded by people claiming to know where she was or what had happened to her. Steve believed it would help the public understand the devastating impact of publicity on families caught in the midst of a tragedy. He also told me that while the family might consider speaking after the trial, they would not go on the record before it. They were terrified of doing anything that might affect the outcome. Still, he offered to speak with them and explore the idea of an informal meeting. I suggested I come to Tennessee ahead of time just to get to know them, with the understanding that any formal interview would take place after the verdict. Though wary of the media, the Bobos trusted Steve. They agreed. I would fly in and meet with them ahead of the trial. After that, they'd decide whether to go forward.

Steve's emphasis on the emotional toll stayed with me. I'd covered many trials. I'd seen the strain on families. But I'd never asked them directly what it was like to endure years of grief while also becoming a public spectacle. How do you survive a tragedy that's playing out on national television? How do you function while the world is speculating about your child's fate—and your own innocence?

In early February 2017, I traveled to Tennessee. Thinking it would be closer, I flew into Nashville instead of Memphis. It turned out both airports were hours from the Bobos' home. I'd been driving nearly three hours when I finally reached the outskirts of Darden. Dusk was settling in. The light was fading. The road narrowed, surrounded by thick woods and rolling hills. I rolled down the window. The air was still and cool. Gravel crunched under my tires as I approached the long driveway. The place felt peaceful, removed—a haven from the chaos of the outside world. It didn't seem like the kind of place where something unspeakable could happen. Karen Bobo met me at the end of the driveway and motioned for me to pull up. She looked younger than I expected: petite, blonde, warm. I apologized for being late, explaining I'd gotten lost. She smiled and said it happened often. As we stepped inside, she introduced me to her husband, Dana. He was quiet, gray-haired, polite. Shy, perhaps, but kind. The kitchen was softly lit, with dark cabinets and neat hand towels stacked by the sink. They offered me something to eat, then led me into the living room.

At the entrance, I noticed a large framed photo of Holly at her high school graduation. Beside it was a photo of her brother, Clint. I stopped. Karen saw me looking. She said, "It's nice to look at this photo. She was so full of happiness. We were best friends." Then she added, "We've kept the house pretty much the way it was when Holly was alive, but we're going to be moving after the trial. It is hard to be here sometimes without her." [4,5]

"She was so beautiful," I said gently, placing a hand on Karen's back. We stepped into the den—wood-paneled, softly lit, with a big black sofa facing the TV. A dog hopped up beside me.

Karen laughed. "This was Holly's dog." She scratched its ears and smiled. Dana settled nearby, listening as Karen spoke. They shared small glances, quiet support. After thirty years together, they still moved like a team.

"I appreciate you letting me into your home," I said. "I want you to know that I'm here to listen. I'm not here to pressure you or sell you anything. I know how much you've endured. I don't want to make it worse."

Karen nodded. "I wish the trial were over already."

"Going to be rough, but we have to get justice for Holly," Dana added.

---

4 Interview with the Bobo Family (Dana and Karen) at their home, February 2, 2017.

5 Phone call conversation with Karen Bobo to discuss the delay in the trial date until July, April 3, 2017.

I explained that this meeting was informal. The real interview would come—if they agreed—after the trial, likely with Elizabeth Vargas.

"Is it okay if I take notes on my laptop?" I asked.

"Fine with the notes," Karen said. "But, just so you know, though, we're not going to be doing anything on TV before the trial. The prosecutor has asked us not to talk to you people."

"Okay. I'm just here to listen. I won't release any of our conversation before the trial."

"Also, sorry that Clint isn't here tonight. He's just not ready to be interviewed," Karen added.

I smiled and said I understood, though I couldn't help wondering if Clint would ever agree to speak with me. My producer was pressuring me for an interview with him—he was the last person to see Holly alive. But I also knew the family's trust would be essential.

"But if you both decide to interview with us, do you think he'll also do one?" I asked hopefully.

"I think so," Karen replied. "You need to understand how hard this has been for Clint. He saw his sister abducted in front of his eyes, and he's blamed himself every day since. Nothing that happened was his fault. And then he was attacked by just about everyone online..."

She went on, describing the fallout—and the damage.

Dana and Karen opened up.

And I listened.

The Private Struggle

Karen's voice was steady, but her eyes betrayed her exhaustion. She told me about how Clint agreed to talk about Holly when she was still missing to keep her abduction in the news. He explained during his interview that he'd thought Holly was with her boyfriend, Drew, when he heard loud voices. He assumed Drew was out turkey hunting and had stopped to visit with Holly.

"We were all doing interviews to try and get people to look for Holly," Karen told me. "Clint agreed to do one with Jane Velez-Mitchell. She's on HLN or something. She was the worst. After he explained it was turkey hunting season to her, she yelled, 'You thought he was Turkey hunting. Turkey hunting? Now, come on!'"

"I've seen her do that to people on her show," I said. "She doesn't know how to use her indoor voice."

Karen nodded grimly.

"The media was so cruel to him, but none of it was as bad as the TBI investigators," Dana interjected.

"They thought from the beginning that Clint had something to do with Holly's kidnapping," Dana explained. "The real problem is that the police go by the statistics, that someone from the home is responsible. I kept telling them, 'We don't fit in your damn statistics.' When word got out that Holly had been abducted, we were at home trying to man the phones alone for hours. There were hundreds of calls coming into the house. We were on those phones long before the FBI arrived. They all appeared to be in their thirties. Before that, it was Karen, Clint, and me trying to take them down. Decatur County sent the first two cops. TBI was next. The first four hours were a cluster, man.

Everybody is saying, 'I am in charge.' You know, say a bank gets robbed, and every cop goes to that bank. That's what happened here. Karen was begging them to block the roads off right after she disappeared. She even lied to them about Holly's age to get an Amber Alert out. I talked to some other folks whose kids had gone missing, and we all agreed, there needs to be something for young adults. There needs to be an Amber Alert when a young adult goes missing."

Karen shook her head; her expression clouded with grief. "It was awful. My mom lived here for more than a year and a half and only went home on the weekends. We slept on the couch in here for nearly a year. She physically took care of me. No one cooked here for months. People were bringing food every day."

Dana explained how, during those early months, he left the house daily to search for Holly, joining up with roughly a hundred others—some familiar, many strangers. These people gave up workdays to help. Dana said he wanted to stop and thank each one, to tell them how much it meant. But he couldn't. He couldn't even speak. He held onto one hope: that Holly had been taken but was still alive, held somewhere, waiting to be found. He prayed she would escape. That she would come home.

"I was off for a couple of months, and my boss paid me," Dana told me. "He called a lot of guys out of jobs and paid them to come and help search for Holly for a month or two. Everybody in the whole town was doing that. Karen wrote books of prayers. There was no daytime or nighttime for months. There was no time anymore. This was weeks after Holly was taken. Leaving the house, some of the people I knew—half of them I knew—and a lot of them had guns. On the weekday when they all should have been at work, they were out helping me search for our daughter.

I wanted to stop and tell everyone and say thank you for searching. I couldn't tell them thank you. I just couldn't talk."

"It was horrible that she was missing, but not as horrible as her being dead," Karen said quietly. "We didn't know what to do. When Holly's phone was found on that Easter Sunday, a few days after she'd gone missing, I went out with Dana in our pickup to search for her. When we came down the hill and stopped there to see if traffic was coming, I saw at least two hundred people out there—everybody on the right side was down on their hands and knees looking for something because her phone was found there. Everyone on the other side was standing up and walking and touching shoulders. That was the first day of going out and searching alone." She looked down. "We were so close. Holly always wanted someone to help. I know that most mothers always say their daughters are the most talented and the most beautiful. But the one thing about Holly, she always picked someone to help. She loved people."

I stared at Karen, trying not to cry. Normally, I keep a professional distance. But in that moment, I couldn't stop thinking about my own daughter—and how impossible this all must be to endure. I excused myself and went to the bathroom to collect myself.

When I returned, Karen was talking about the early days of media frenzy. "After Holly disappeared, the news media were all over us. Everyone was calling. It was crazy. This woman, Sheila, contacted us and said she was a private detective and she could help us find Holly. When we were about to interview with her, she said, 'Karen, you can't wear black. That makes you look dishonest. You need to wear blue.' It was crazy. I don't think she hurt anything, but she used us. We've been used so many times.

And that website Topix talked terribly about Clint, and he got death threats."

Their pain wasn't limited to the media. They'd also lost faith in law enforcement. "The TBI always seemed to be behind because they refused to seriously investigate anyone besides the Bobos," Karen said. "The investigation was incompetent from the start. They refused to issue an Amber Alert because Holly was twenty. I ended up lying to them that Holly was younger, so they'd do it. Did you know that they also messed up tracking Holly's phone? It was pinging for forty-five minutes as she was busy being driven away. They could have gotten to her, but they missed the chance."

"It was a damn mess," Dana agreed.

"There was an investigator in Decatur County that I didn't trust—the sheriff, Ricky Inman," Karen continued. "I asked TBI not to put him on the case. And naturally, that's who they ended up putting on it. Every time they found some evidence against the folks I suspected from the start—the local boy Shane Austin or the Adams boys who live right nearby—this Sheriff Ricky would turn away from these people and say it wasn't them. He was the sheriff for Decaturville, and believe it or not, he's now the head of the police department. He led the TBI investigators to Terry Britt, and that's partly why we thought Terry Britt wasn't involved in the kidnapping. He ignored the real suspects and inserted himself into the investigation." Then her voice shifted. "One night, after everyone had left, we were alone in the house. We grew up together, so I've known him for most of my life. He nicknamed me Twinkles. So that night, he says, 'Twinkles, I want you to stop blaming yourself.' And I told him, 'Ricky, I'm not blaming myself.' And he kept saying it. 'Stop blaming yourself. Stop blaming yourself, Twinkles.' He was trying to make me kill myself."

I sat frozen. I didn't know what to say.

"One day, he even called me at school," Karen said. "He asked me to come by his office. He said that he had pictures that I'd never seen. He got up from his desk, put his hand on my knee, and said it again, 'Twinkles, you need to stop blaming yourself.' I was so angry. Ricky had so many chances to catch Holly's killers—the three of them—Jason Autry, the Adams brothers, and Shane Austin. Ricky had stopped Zach Adams with drugs and then just let him go. Ricky also had a nickname for Jason Autry—called him Train. I mean, unless you are friends with someone, how would you know their nickname? When I suggested that Jason Autry might be involved in Holly's abduction, Ricky would say, 'Train wouldn't do nothing like this.' He also called those four—the two Adams brothers, Autry, and Shane Austin—the four on the 'A' train because those four were always together. Those four were the ones. I knew it from the beginning."

A Mother's Investigation

Two years after Holly's abduction, the family got a call from the TBI. Holly's pink purse had been found on the side of a road. Ricky Inman brought a photo to the Bobo house. But Karen took one look and said it wasn't Holly's.

"They wanted it to be Holly's purse because, under their theory, if it was found in a neighbor's yard, it was likely that Clint was involved," she told me. "They wanted to bring the whole thing back to us...and Clint. They kept refusing to let me see the actual purse. And the more I said it wasn't Holly's purse, the angrier they got at me. They were friends with this Jason Autry, and they were protecting him."

I asked about TBI agent Terry Dicus, the only investigator the family trusted for a time. Dicus had long believed Terry Britt, a local sex offender, was responsible. Britt had a record for kidnapping and rape and lived near the Bobos. But Karen didn't think he was the one.

"Dicus told me that dogs hit on human remains when they searched his house," I said.

Dana interjected quickly. "I was at every search, and no cadaver dogs hit on anything in Terry Britt's house or yard. We had one dog hit near a pond. Little shallow pond and had nothing to do with Terry Britt. Dicus is wrong."

Karen and Dana described the three years they spent in limbo—waiting, hoping, investigating leads on their own. At one point, they reached out to Ed Smart, Elizabeth Smart's father, hoping for guidance.

"We are just telling you a little of what we've been through," Karen explained. "Elizabeth Smart came and did a talk at Holly's high school. Ed and Elizabeth came down and met us at the hospital. I spoke to him on the phone several times. The last time I talked to him, he told me that Elizabeth had gotten married. Things with us were bad. Clint went through a breakdown last Christmas, in 2017. He got married in June 2015. He was building a house on my mom's property, down around where Drew was turkey hunting on the morning of Holly's abduction.

"Just a few weeks after Holly was taken, we were outside washing Holly's car," she told me. "It was green from all the pollen. We were outside, and this guy just stopped by—a farmer who lived near us. He told us about seeing Shane Austin on Friday or Saturday at this adult bookstore with scratches on his face. I was hearing the names of those four killers were getting to me real early on."

Karen learned that Holly had crossed paths with Shane Austin shortly before her disappearance. She and her boyfriend, Drew, had gone coon hunting, and a friend later reported that a strange man had followed Holly around that night. That friend, Candice, called Karen after Holly went missing.

"Holly never told me about someone following her," Karen said. "But when I found out, I asked Candice to talk to a sketch artist. The TBI gave us a copy of the sketch. Dana's cousin was here that night, and he viewed the sketch and was positive it looked like Shane Austin. I decided to find him and talk to him."

Karen's method was simple and gut-driven. "I felt that if I could just shake the hand of someone I suspected, I would know if they took Holly. When I was doing my investigating, I would talk to the person I suspected for a bit, and then when I was leaving, I'd shake their hand."

When she met Shane Austin, his parents were present. "When I was done talking to Shane Austin, I shook his hand, and it was sweaty and clammy. His mom was crying and sobbing the whole time. And I knew then that he was involved, and I think his mama knew too. Shane ended up hanging himself in an apartment or motel in Florida. Some people say he could have gotten forgiveness before he did that. I say if he'd gotten forgiveness before that, he'd have left a note. I believe if he'd felt enough guilt, he'd have left a note. I think he hung himself because he didn't want to face the consequences. TBI was questioning everybody. He was next on the list, and he was working in Florida."

After Autry and the Adams brothers were arrested, investigators approached Shane Austin. At first, he denied any involvement. Eventually, prosecutors offered him immunity in exchange for information. The deal protected him from being charged in connection with concealing, disposing of, or burying Holly's body and granted him immunity for drug-related offenses—except those involving drugs given to Holly. But the agreement hinged on Austin telling authorities where Holly's remains were. When he failed to do so, the state moved to void the deal and attempted to indict him on two separate occasions. Austin fled to Florida and took his own life. Karen and Dana believed that guilt drove him to suicide.

Later, I interviewed Shane Austin's attorney, Luke Evans, in Murfreesboro. He wouldn't discuss privileged conversations but insisted Shane was not involved in Holly's disappearance. He blamed the suicide on personal issues and public scrutiny.

I listened. I didn't quite believe him.

Karen also suspected Jason Autry early on, but she didn't know where to find him—until a friend spotted him at a grocery store. She didn't hesitate.

"I introduced myself, and the first thing he said was that he wanted to know how his name came up in all of this. He claimed that he didn't know Holly and that he'd heard Karen's son was involved." Karen shook her head, clearly still incredulous. "This guy had on khaki cargo shorts and flip flops. We talked for a bit, and I knew he was involved. I shook his hand when we got ready to walk away, and he instantly got cold chills all over his body. Even his nipples got hard. As soon as I got back into the car, I called all four TBI agents and told them everything that had happened during our conversation with Jason. I didn't want to hide anything from them. The TBI wasn't happy we were out there doing their job, but I knew something wasn't right with him."

After Autry's arrest for murder, Karen went to talk to his father because he was Dana's third cousin. Jason's father and Dana were friends when they were young and often ran around together.

"He said that Jason had written them some letters from prison and asked if I wanted to read them," Karen recalled. "He said he finds Jesus when he goes to prison and loses him when he gets out. He said sometimes he thinks Jason is involved and sometimes he thinks he's not, but he knew how mean Autry is."

Dana interjected, "If he knew Autry took Holly, he would have told us."

"Well, his mother will cover it up until the end," Karen shot back.

Eventually, Karen sought out Zach Adams too. She'd taught him in school and knew his family. In July 2011, she, Dana, and Clint drove to Zach's house. No one answered the door. They went to the main house, where Zach's grandfather and brother Dylan lived. Karen left her phone number with Dylan and asked him to have Zach call.

The next day, he did.

"I am not sure he ever sat down," Karen told me. "He was nervous. His voice was low one minute and loud the next. I don't remember a whole lot of what he said, but two things stood out to me right then. He asked Clint to describe the person who took Holly. After Clint was done, he said, 'That person was Shane.'"

The Discovery

Three years after Holly disappeared, the call finally came.

"It was on a Sunday," Karen told me. "We were checking out at the American Eagle store. My phone rang, and the police told me that her remains had been found in northern Decatur County. They said we won't be getting her remains until after the investigation and trial are over. It was so awful. We still don't have her remains and can't lay her to rest. I saw the Casey Anthony story where they didn't bury that baby until after the trial. They recommended not burying Holly. We felt there was never going to be full closure. There is nothing these guys can say; there is no one who can make me understand why this had to happen to our daughter. Why her? You can ask the question, but you can't get an answer. Nothing that they can ever say can answer that question. I hate them."

She handed me one of the prayer journals she'd kept. "When I wrote those prayers in the books every night after she was gone, I wrote, 'Please God, don't let her get weak.' I felt that she could feel me telling her to stay strong. In 2014, I was still begging God to let her live. I was sure she was alive."

The pages were filled front and back with pleading, raw prayers.

"When they found her remains, I got mad and threw some of them away," she admitted. "It was just so hard. I probably had ten journals and threw over half of them away. I started to throw away the Bible, but I just couldn't."

Clint continued to struggle. He'd recently married, and the Bobos were building him a home on family land. That first Christmas after Holly's death, they tried to return to some sense of normalcy. It didn't work.

"That Christmas affected the whole family," Karen said during my interview with her and Dana. "We were torn up. It was too soon. I learned that you have to create a whole new normalcy because you can't go back, and you can't rush it. People say, 'Oh, you should be doing this or doing that.' No, you do things when it feels right."[6] [7]

"There is no book on how to get back to your new normal," Dana added. "You try to stay the man of the family, and that's what I tried to do, but our roles kind of changed. I was the man of the house. But when I went back to work and Karen didn't, Karen had to work on looking for Holly every day. We switched roles almost. I kind of let her take over the role of the man. You couldn't care less about what anyone thinks about you."

Three months after Holly's remains were discovered, a Decatur County grand jury indicted Zach Adams for especially aggravated kidnapping, rape, and first-degree murder. Jason Autry was indicted a month later, followed by Dylan Adams. Zach and Autry had long criminal records. Just nine days before Holly's abduction, Zach Adams was arrested on charges of tampering with evidence, assaulting an officer, drug possession, and resisting arrest. He was released on a $12,500 bond. He was arrested again in June 2011 for driving on a suspended license. Autry's record included drug and theft convictions.

Then came a false lead: brothers Jeffrey and Mark Pearcy were arrested after rumors surfaced that they possessed a video

6 Interview with the Bobo Family (Dana and Karen) at their home, February 2, 2017.

7 Phone call conversation with Karen Bobo to discuss the delay in the trial date until July, April 3, 2017.

showing Holly tied up and crying. But there was no video. The charges were dismissed.

Meanwhile, prosecutors announced they had sworn statements from two witnesses who said they saw Adams and Autry with Holly while she was still alive. Adams was also charged with coercion. The intense publicity prompted defense lawyers to request a change of venue, arguing their clients couldn't get a fair trial in Decatur County.

As trial preparations continued, I returned to Tennessee to investigate new leads. A source close to Dylan Adams agreed to meet me privately, far from Darden. The source alleged that Dylan had the mental capacity of a child—with an IQ in the low seventies—and could not understand the charges against him. He had been placed in a so-called "safe house" after a federal arrest, allegedly to facilitate a confession.

The charge? Possessing and disposing of a stolen firearm. According to the source, the gun belonged to someone else—Jason Kilzer—and the feds only targeted Dylan to pressure him about the Bobo case. Court records revealed that Dylan was later released into the custody of a former law enforcement official, who brought him back in to confess. The confession was recorded on video. In it, Dylan implicated Zach Adams, Jason Autry, and Shane Austin.

I contacted Jennifer Thompson, attorney for both Adams brothers. She agreed to speak.

She told me Dylan's confession had been coerced. "It was obvious from the video that Dylan didn't understand the questions and that the police led him to certain answers," she said. "He told investigators that when it was his turn with Holly, he'd raped her repeatedly for four hours. But it was all false."

She claimed the confession was riddled with inaccuracies—and yet formed the basis of the case against Zach. She declined to share the video, but I eventually obtained it from another source. After watching it, I had to admit: her analysis held weight. Dylan appeared confused, passive, and often repeated what was suggested to him.

When we spoke again, Thompson pointed out something troubling: "The state swore out a warrant for the Bobo family's banking records in January 2013." The warrant, signed by Judge C. Creed McGinley, claimed the records were needed to track the family's movements during Holly's disappearance.

Thompson believed both the Adams brothers were innocent—and that the real killer was Terry Britt. "When they found Holly's remains, they found several bones of Holly, not the lower half of her body. By the way, a man named Terry Britt bought a chainsaw two weeks after Holly disappeared," she said.

"But weren't the remains found close to the Adams' property?" I asked.

"No. It wasn't necessarily close to the Adams' property," Thompson replied. "Holly's home is closer to Terry Britt's than the Adams' property. The TBI searched Britt's property. He had a shovel, an axe, and two hammers, and the cadaver dogs hit on that. They also hit on two of his vehicles. They found a long blonde hair that they were going to test further. I haven't been able to figure out where those tests are."

She claimed that without Dylan's confession, the TBI had no real case—only their original theory, which had targeted Clint Bobo.

"They put a recording device in Dylan's jail cell and sent in his co-defendant from the federal case to pump him for information," she said. "Then they questioned Dylan for hours without his lawyer present. They manipulated the sibling rivalry between the brothers. Dylan is speculating in that video. The investigator made him say that he walked into his brother's house and saw a blonde woman on the couch, and Zach told him to leave."

Thompson also doubted Jason Autry's credibility. "He'd already confessed," she noted. "The TBI was so hard on him that he opted to work out a deal and come up with a new story that would help them convict Zach and Dylan. They're abandoning Dylan's false confession and going with Jason's false confession."

I later met Dylan and Zach's mother, Cindy Adams. She also believed Dylan's confession was coerced. She described him as unable to speak clearly or understand much without help.

"He always attended special schools," she said. Both sons were drug addicts, but she insisted neither was a killer. Her defense of Dylan was unwavering, but when it came to Zach, things were more complicated.

When Zach was nineteen, he shot Cindy with a nine-millimeter Glock after she refused to give him money for drugs. She got a restraining order. He pleaded guilty to assault and received a jail sentence of eleven months and twenty-nine days, which was suspended after six months so he could attend rehab. The judge who presided? C. Creed McGinley—the same man who would later oversee Zach's murder trial.

The Other Suspects

As I continued reviewing motions and transcripts and speaking with sources, one pattern became undeniable: even long after

Dylan Adams's confession and the arrests of the three defendants, many in law enforcement still viewed Clint Bobo as a suspect. According to public records and defense filings, the TBI had tapped Clint's phones, monitored the family's internet use, and obtained warrants for the Bobos' computers. All this occurred before the remains were discovered. Most TBI agents rejected the theory held by one of their own—Special Agent Terry Dicus.

Dicus believed that Clint had nothing to do with Holly's disappearance. He also believed that the state was prosecuting the wrong men. Eventually, his superiors grew frustrated with his refusal to abandon his theory that Terry Britt was responsible. Dicus was removed from the case. But that didn't stop him from cooperating with the defense. When I learned that Dicus would testify on behalf of Zach Adams, I contacted him. He agreed to speak with me.

Dicus remained firm. He believed that Britt, a convicted sexual predator, was the one who had taken Holly. "Britt had stalked a lot of women who looked exactly like Holly," Dicus told me. "Holly was his type." Britt's criminal history supported the profile. He had been convicted of kidnapping and rape and was known to prey on young women in the area. When asked to take a polygraph about Holly's case, Britt refused.

Dicus pointed to cell phone data showing that Britt's phone had pinged on the same road as Holly's around the time she disappeared. More chilling, Dicus said, were the accounts of two loggers working near the Bobo home that morning. The loggers reported seeing a white male with "feathery" black hair wearing a black cap, driving alongside a blonde woman in a pink shirt, just like the one Holly had been wearing that day. The woman's face was obscured, her head bent down. The witnesses were never able to positively identify the man or the girl in the truck. Still, Dicus believed it was them.

The theory opened the case wide. On one side were investigators and prosecutors who had charged Zach, Dylan, and Autry—basing much of their case on Dylan's controversial confession and Autry's later testimony. On the other hand, Dicus maintained that Terry Britt, not the Adams brothers, had committed the crime. And in between were the Bobos, still searching for truth, still surrounded by doubt, grief, and a community eager for answers.

CHAPTER THREE

The Jury Is Finally Seated

Even though Holly Bobo's remains were found in September of 2014, the trial of Zach Adams was initially set for April 2017. However, after a change of venue was granted, it was postponed until September 2017. Zachary Adams stood trial for Holly's abduction, rape, and murder, along with Jason Autry. His brother, John Dylan Adams, would be tried later.

Although I already knew the Bobo family and had met with Zach and Dylan's mother, I didn't meet Clint Bobo until the first day of trial. When I approached the Bobos to say hello, Karen greeted me but noted that she wasn't supposed to be talking to me. The prosecutor had learned of our earlier meeting and was worried it might influence the trial. I reassured Karen that nothing from our meeting would be discussed until after the verdict. She nodded, and we didn't speak again until the trial was over.

The courtroom was spacious, its wooden benches filled with family, friends, and spectators. The front rows on the right, closest to the jury, were occupied by Holly's family and supporters.

They sat together, occasionally turning to greet new arrivals. I sat in the center with a clear view of the witness stand. Steve Farese, the Bobos' attorney, sat beside me, yellow pad in hand.

The pool camera, shared by all media outlets, was placed discreetly in the back corner, positioned to avoid capturing the jury. Down the hall, a media room streamed the proceedings, offering reporters a space to speak freely and file their stories. Inside the courtroom, however, we were expected to remain silent and expressionless. Meanwhile, sheriff's deputies watched me and the rest of the press like hawks. Even a simple greeting to Dana and Karen Bobo was met with a stern reprimand and veiled threats of removal. Later, a quiet comment to a colleague got me relegated to the back row.

Judge McGinley quickly established his authority, warmly engaging with the jury and making light conversation. Zach Adams, expressionless and quiet, glanced around but showed no emotion, no interaction with his mother. He seemed utterly alone.

Opening Statements

Prosecutor Paul Hagerman began with a gentle, barely audible tone that nearly lulled the courtroom to sleep. When I whispered to Steve asking if he could hear Hagerman, a deputy immediately shushed me. We both leaned a tad forward on the bench, struggling to hear him.

Hagerman began by painting a portrait of Holly Bobo as a bright, kind nursing student preparing for a test on the morning she disappeared. He outlined the prosecution's theory: Adams kidnapped Holly, drugged and raped her, then called Jason Autry to help dispose of her body. Hagerman alleged that Holly was still alive when they went to move her body, but Adams, determined not to leave a witness, shot her in the head.

Jason Autry, according to Hagerman, would testify to witnessing the murder. Hagerman said other witnesses would testify that Adams confessed and bragged about killing Holly. Despite the lack of physical evidence, Hagerman promised the jury they would hear compelling testimony.

Defense attorney Jennifer Thompson opened by declaring Zach Adams innocent, stressing that he did not know Holly Bobo and had never seen her. She emphasized the lack of evidence: five hundred items were taken from Adams's home, four cars searched, and phone records analyzed—none of which linked him to the crime. She reminded the jury that the TBI had at one point focused on the Bobo family itself. She warned that Autry's testimony came in exchange for avoiding the death penalty and argued that his story conveniently filled the gaps left by the state's lack of evidence.

The first witnesses included Dana and Clint Bobo, but Karen Bobo's testimony was the most emotional. Listening to her 911 call, she sobbed quietly, her shoulders shaking. When prosecutor John Nichols showed her Holly's purse, she broke down. "It looks like her purse. That is her purse…that's her purse," she confirmed tearfully. [8]

When Nichols asked her to identify more items—Holly's license, insurance card, student ID—Karen trembled. As he placed Holly's wallet on the projector and asked her to check for a

---

[8] The trial testimony of Karen Bobo is taken from my notes as well as from pool coverage of the trial later posted by Law and Crime on YOUTUBE https://www.youtube.com/watch?v=31w8b5NrQHs&list=PLoW1SIeAWaWbNG-RXiqJeKy2ZWK_JTlb4&index=5

twenty-dollar bill she'd left inside, she answered, "No, there is nothing in it." Suddenly, she gasped. "Hang on just a minute, I'm feeling sick." She then collapsed on the witness stand.

"Get a nurse and get some lights. Clerk, lights!" Judge McGinley shouted.

Karen lay on the floor, gasping. "I can't breathe," she said. Minutes later, pale but upright, she was helped from the stand. The defense moved for a mistrial, arguing the jury had been prejudiced by the dramatic scene. But Judge McGinley denied the motion, stating firmly that Karen had suffered a real medical event, not a staged display for sympathy.

Jason Autry didn't testify until the fourth day. His appearance was unsettling: a large man with greasy hair and prison garb who exuded menace. He seemed intelligent, confident, and disturbingly comfortable on the stand. His testimony was detailed and almost *too* consistent. It felt rehearsed. I understood why the prosecution had cut a deal with him. They needed a witness to tell the jury what happened to Holly Bobo; Zach Adams had refused to make a deal, and Autry was clearly the more sophisticated of the two. Autry seemed like a leader with a commanding presence about him. He didn't seem like someone who would agree to do Zach Adams's bidding.

He took the stand at 10:30 a.m., having spent the night in the Henderson County jail. Autry had been raised in Parsons, Tennessee, where he spent sixteen years before he moved to the city. He'd been arrested four times, three of those times for theft and drug-related crimes, and now, for murder. Autry sat on the witness stand, seemingly at ease as he began to testify that he'd known Zach Adams for fifteen years, as well as his brother, Dylan. He'd met their father through a drug deal. He also revealed that he was a cousin of Shane Austin, another man implicated in Holly's abduction. Autry said that the night before Holly was kidnapped, he had spent the night with his girlfriend, Angela.[9]

Autry testified that on the day of Holly's abduction, he got into the truck and went to Camden Bottom, a large refuge, to kill some time looking at the wildlife and feeding the ducks and the deer. He was waiting to get hold of a drug dealer to get his fix. "I am a country boy. I enjoy the sights and scenery…I wanted to make a phone call and establish a connection on morphine." He explained that he was addicted to morphine, methamphetamine, and hydrocodone. "I started a volley of exchanges to Shane Austin and Mr. Adams." He didn't care who answered his call first."

I sat up in my chair, listening to Autry. He seemed articulate, calm and fairly intelligent. He painted a picture of himself as a drug addict who was looking to just get drugs the day that Holly was abducted. He liked to have a cocktail of morphine and meth in the morning, but on April 11, he only had the meth and needed the morphine. Zach Adams called Autry back at around 8:40 a.m. and said to come and meet him at Shane Austin's house—Autry's cousin who lived on Yellow Springs Road.

Autry recalled Adams saying, "I need to see you, I need your help…" Autry told the jury that he had no idea what kind of help Adams needed but speculated that maybe a bad batch of meth was messed up.

---

9. Jason Autry's testimony is taken from my copious trial notes as well as from pool camera footage that is now on YOUTUBE at https://www.youtube.com/watch?v=TgsMhNbUHxA&list=PLoW1SIeAWaWbNG-RXiqJeKy2ZWK_JTlb4&index=10; Part TWO https://www.youtube.com/watch?v=NikLr4FGEKA&list=PLoW1SIeAWaWbNG-RXiqJeKy2ZWK_JTlb4&index=11

"When I pulled into his driveway, I got out, and the first thing there was a large fire burning in a burn barrel," Autry explained. "Dylan Adams was standing in the door of the trailer with his shirt off. Shane was walking around in the yard, saying, 'You all need to hurry up and get the God Damn hell out of here' with a firearm holstered on the right side. Zach was standing at the door of a white Nissan Frontier. I instantly got to Mr. Austin and bought a peel, bought a morphine one hundred milligram, and walked directly back to the PT cruiser, broke it in half, cooked it down, and shot it. A few minutes later, I got out and walked back to the four-by-four Nissan, where Zach was standing at the door."[10]

Zach told Autry that he needed his help to bury this body. "And I said, God Damn, I hate that you all killed little Jo Jo. And he said, 'Train'—my nickname is Train—'that's Holly Bobo.'"

The stenographer asked Autry to repeat his answer; she'd not heard him. He repeated himself, barely changing a word of his previous response. The effect was unsettling. It seemed that he was going through a well-rehearsed script, carefully written to include all the relevant details, with no regard for how it made him appear. I wondered if he even knew how inhuman he sounded. It was clear that he'd been well rehearsed. He would say the same phrases on cross-examination.

"Let's be honest," Nichols said coldly. "Did you care one way or another about the body in the back of the truck?"

"I did not," Autry said coldly.

---

[10] Jason Autry testimony at the trial of Zach Adams in Savannah, Tennessee, courtroom on September 14, 2017.

"Describe for the jury where the body was and what you did after that?" Nichols asked.

"The body was lying in a multicolored farm-style blanket. It looked like multiple colors. Wrapped in the blanket, lying up against the back.... He asked me if I would help him bury the body, and I said, 'Yeah, I will.' But I said, 'I want to leave my car somewhere else besides here. I don't want Shane or Dylan to know that I got involved in this.' I told him, 'Meet me at Yellow Springs Church. I will park the PT Cruiser there, and I'll get in the truck with you.'" According to Autry, Shane stayed behind to wait for a repair guy to install a satellite.

"As we got going down the road," Autry continued, "I brought it to his attention that there were no shovels or pickaxes in the truck. How are we going to bury a body with no shovels or pickaxes? He looks at me like he's lost. And I said I don't know of anywhere a man can just pull up and just get a shovel and pickaxes with a dead body in the vehicle.... I told him that some years back, I had been under the Interstate 40 bridge, and there was a body floating, and I said the only thing holding the body up was the intestines." He paused, waiting for a question. "And we set a course in that direction."

"Why did you mention a body floating? What did you talk about specifically? What was your plan for disposing of Holly's body?" Nichols asked.

"Was to gut her and put her in the deep end of the pool. I told him, I said, 'You put her in the deep end of that slew, turtles and shit will eat her up. Just like that.'"

The court reporter interjected. She hadn't heard his answer. "Turtles and what?"

"Turtles. Animals of opportunity," Autry explained, seemingly pleased to be educating the jury about the topic. He seemed oblivious that he was talking about animals eating Holly's dead body. Nichols tried to interrupt, but Autry continued his lecture. "The only thing holding the other body up was the gases and the guts. It was floating, just like...you see a dead fish, the only thing holding it up are the gases and the intestines. You get the guts out, down it goes." Autry seemed proud that he'd come up with the best way to get rid of Holly's body.

Autry and Adams drove to an area near the Tennessee River and scoped it out for boats and people.

"I got out of the truck with my right hand, and I grabbed the upper torso of Miss Bobo. Zach comes around and lets the tailgate down. I brought the upper torso to the end of the tailgate, where he grabbed the legs, and I set the head, the upper end, on the rip rap pile. In the bed of the truck, there appeared to be a small amount of blood.... The bed of the truck had ridges, and it looked as if it had just lightly skidded over. And the blanket, at the upper end of the torso that I grabbed, had a small blood spot, maybe the size of an orange."

I glanced at Steve Farese, my expression a mix of horror and disgust. He looked back at me, telegraphing that he'd heard Autry call Holly Bobo's body "it." He'd heard others before talk about their victims that way. I had not. My stomach turned a bit with the realization that this man was lacking basic human emotions. I'd read about sociopaths and psychopaths, but I'd never knowingly been so close to one. Autry didn't even pretend to care or show any signs of remorse when he spoke about Holly's head as "the head," as if she were some doll to be discarded on a pile of rocks.

Autry continued his testimony in the same detached and matter-of-fact way. "I grabbed the blanket and walked to the tailgate of the truck. Mr. Adams goes to the driver's side of the pickup, and I'm standing over the top of it with my hands on my knees. At that time, I saw the foot move, a movement, and a sound of distress. It sounded like 'hmm,' sounded like it came from the blanket. At that time, I walked to the door, the passenger side door of the pickup, and Mr. Adams was digging in a fanny pack. And I told him, 'This fucking bitch is still alive.' We just stopped for a second and walked to the front of the truck, and I told Zach, 'She's heard my name called and heard me talking and all.' At that time, he wheels around and walks back to the driver's side pickup, pulls up the floorboard, and takes out a pistol, the same pistol that was holstered on Mr. Austin's side. I said, 'Whoa.'"

"Let me ask you something. Did you say 'whoa' because you thought you were going to save her life and stop him from doing something bad? Or did you say 'whoa' for another reason?" Nichols asked, knowing that this man was only concerned about himself. He'd likely never done anything to help someone else.

Autry replied that he wanted to be sure no one was watching them before Zach shot Holly. He went under the bridge to keep watch, and when he ascertained that no one was coming, he let Adams know.

"And at that time, boom, the gun went off. It sounded to me that it shot three times underneath that bridge. Just one shot, but it echoed underneath that bridge. When the gun went off, martins went off everywhere. Bridge birds. Bird went everywhere, all from under that bridge," Autry said, failing to understand the horror of his description. "And then just dead silence for just a second. And I heard a boat crank up, a boat running somewhere. I took off running, ran back over to the truck, and I told him, 'God damn, we've been seen or heard.' Mr. Adams grabs the feet, and I grab the same spot on the upper torso. The blood spot was probably the size of a grapefruit at that time. We load the body back into the truck, in the same fashion, shut the tailgate, a tear out of there like wild Indians. We set a course back. I look at my cell phone and I say, I need to get the hell to Benton County and meet Angela for lunch."[11]

I looked at Steve again and whispered, "Well, you don't want to kill someone to get in the way of having lunch with your girlfriend." He schooled his face to remain expressionless, but he knew, as I did, that Jason Autry was likely the mastermind behind Holly's abduction, rape, and murder. I felt sick that he'd be free after this trial because he'd been the first to cut a deal with the prosecution.

According to Autry, things between Zach and Shane became tense later that afternoon. Autry needed more morphine and drove to see Zach around 2:30 p.m.

"When I pulled up, the air was thick with animosity," Autry continued. "Shane, Zach, and Dylan were standing outside. You could tell there'd been some fighting and anger amongst them. We got in the truck, and I got on the passenger side, Austin got in the middle, and Mr. Adams got in the driver's seat. There wasn't a word said for thirty-five or forty seconds. Dylan was in the back. Three in the front, one in the back. From Zach's house

---

[11] The testimony of Jason Autry is based on my trial notes as well as my watching the trial years later on YouTube to ensure that my notes were correct. https://www.youtube.com/watch?v=NikLr4FGEKA&list=PLoW1SIeAWaWbNG-RXiqJeKy2ZWK_JTlb4&index=11

to Dottie's house, where we were headed, is less than two miles. We got in there and pulled out of the driveway, and Zach and Shane started arguing.

"Shane told him, 'You didn't have to kill her.' And Zach told him, 'You're just as damn guilty that you hit it.' Zach told him to shut his fucking mouth, that he was sick of discussing it, and then Zach hit Shane."

At Zach's request, Autry met up with Zach and Dylan two days later in a wooded area about a quarter of a mile from the Marathon gas station. They smoked meth, and then Autry questioned him. "I said, 'What did you ever do with the old girl?'" He told Autry that they'd thrown her out over near Kelly Ridge, but that wasn't why he wanted to meet up with Autry. He was concerned about Dylan, who'd not slept in days and who was constantly talking about what they'd done. He offered Autry money if he would get rid of Dylan.

Moments later, I stood and watched warily as Autry was led out of the courtroom by several deputies. He seemed relaxed and glanced freely around the courtroom, arrogant with a bit of a smirk. He felt in control, and he was enjoying reliving the events surrounding poor Holly Bobo's death. I was on my way to the ladies' restroom when we locked eyes, and I felt chilled. I felt the presence of palpable evil. I'd interviewed a lot of killers, but there was something about Autry that made him different. He thought he was smarter than everyone—the prosecutors, the defense lawyers, and naturally, the Adams brothers. He was going to be set free while they either were executed or spent the rest of their young lives in prison. More than anyone I've ever met, Jason Autry was a predator. He wasn't the kind of man who rushed under a bridge to be a lookout while someone else committed murder. He was the kind of man to do it himself.

After the break, Autry returned to the stand, testifying about how Zach had offered him a portion of the money that he would inherit after his grandfather passed if he would kill Dylan. Zach sweetened the offer by also telling Autry that he was free to stay in one of the houses on the Adams' property after Dylan was gone.

"I told him that it was something I needed to think about, and that I wasn't prepared to do it today. He told me if I decided to do that, to let him know. And I told him when I get done with that, you'll probably be next.... Meaning, I was probably going to kill him too. I felt like after I'd evaluated the situation.... I felt like in my heart, he should have notified me and let me know before he brought me into a situation like that.... I felt that I was brought into that."

A few days later, Autry informed Zach that he'd kill Dylan. Autry surprised Dylan at home, got him stoned, and then lured him into going fishing. Autry's boating trip with Dylan ended with both men getting high and drunk, with Autry ready to murder Dylan, but he had to abandon the plan at the last minute because they were spotted by another boat.

Autry explained to the jury that a year later, in August 2012, he and Zach Adams were out riding around and went to Eagle Creek in Camden, Tennessee. They stopped and took a couple of hits off a meth pipe. Autry said that he turned to Zach and said, "Looks like we got by with this shit. [We were] talking about the kidnapping, rape, and murder of Holly Bobo. I asked him at that time how a man allows himself to rape someone with two other men watching, and he [Zach] said Dylan sucked him off.

Got him hard. And I told him, 'That's sick, nasty man.' No fine details. I let it be known that I don't stand for that shit."

As his direct testimony came to an end, Autry discussed the months that followed Holly's disappearance. Autry admitted that although he'd lied to law enforcement, the media, and his mother about his part in the Bobo case, he was telling the truth now. I looked around the jury, wondering if they believed him. They were listening intently and seemed in a weird way to like Autry. He'd testified to the jurors as if they were friends, playing up his country routes, and casting himself as the misguided drug addict who accidentally got involved in murdering Holly. He employed charm; calculated, self-deprecating humor; and doses of faux humility.

Just before the cross-examination was set to begin, Steve Farese and I took our seats. I told Steve about my earlier encounter with Autry in the hallway and the bad feeling he'd given me. Steve nodded, his expression unreadable since we were back in the courtroom. He grabbed my yellow pad and wrote, "Sounds like he did his job." I nodded, my expression completely readable.

"He killed her," I whispered. "I am sure of it."

Steve grabbed my pad again and wrote, "Really. He seems like such a good guy."

I read his note and said in my usual stage whisper, "He is a psychopath."

Just as Steve was about to respond, Judge McGinley approached us, bringing our conversation to a close. Steve introduced me as his journalist friend, carefully omitting any other identifying details. The judge smiled and made some quip about me behaving myself, and I pretended to laugh. The judge chatted with Steve, laughing about some of the outrageous tactics that Steve had employed over the years in various murder trials. The two laughed and teased one another as they chatted. The judge teased Steve, saying that if he'd tried to pull some of his stunts in his court, Steve wouldn't have gotten away with it. Steve smiled but said nothing as he shook the judge's hand.

I wrote on my pad, "His hair is awfully black."

Steve wrote back, "It's natural." I tried not to laugh, but failed. Everyone looked over at me. The sheriff shook his finger in my direction.

Court resumed with the cross-examination of Jason Autry. Right from the beginning, Jennifer Thompson's cross-examination of Jason Autry was belabored and contentious. Thompson told Autry she wanted to go back through his version of events, prompting Autry to agree. After every question Thompson asked, he waited a beat before answering at a glacial pace.

They first got into a back-and-forth about the fact that Zach Adams wasn't the first call that Mr. Thompson made that morning. Thompson continued with her cross, pointing out that Autry had been very clear and precise in his testimony about calling Mr. Adams first thing that morning. Thompson got Autry to admit that he called Angela Scott before speaking to Mr. Adams and that he'd mischaracterized the nature of his job. It demonstrated that Autry had been unclear about the events, but Autry was apologetic. It was a harbinger of what was to come.

When Thompson asked about text messages that morning, Autry again admitted that he'd testified incorrectly, admitting that he'd texted Zach first that morning instead of calling him first. Again, Thompson seemed triumphant.

"So, it's a fact that you don't remember so clearly," Thompson said before grabbing another exhibit.

"I don't think the state asked every call that I made that day," Autry replied before adding, "The prosecutor was very precise in every question she asked." The obvious implication was that Thompson was not, and the jury got it and struggled not to laugh.

Things for Thompson got worse when she questioned Autry about the various routes he took on the day of the murder. She was trying to show that it would have been impossible, time-wise, for him to drive to all those places. However, after some difficulty, she posted a map on the overhead projector that was missing some of the roads that Autry had referred to in his direct testimony. He kept telling her that the maps were incomplete and told the jury that sometimes he took back roads, as he'd grown up in the area. The jury smiled, amused by Autry and annoyed by Thompson's inability to find his route on the map. She finally handed a map to Autry, asking him to identify his route, but he struggled with it as well, noting that key roads were unmarked and that one map didn't even show the road where Shane Austin lived. While he wasn't rude, he waited patiently, literally smiling at the jury as the papers on her podium scattered to the floor. At one point, he instructed Thompson to find another map that had the route to Shane Austin's house on it.

"We need a map with south of Interstate 40," he said, seemingly stunned by her incompetence.

Steve Farese, a maestro at cross-examination, listened to Thompson's cross-examination with a pained expression. It was like watching a car accident; I wanted to look away, but couldn't. He scribbled a funny critique of Jennifer Thompson on my yellow pad that summed up the real-time disaster unfolding.

Thompson passed Autry exhibit number two.

"This is after we got into the vehicle and headed toward the alleged 'dump site.' This map is our tracks after I got in," Autry explained.

Thompson nodded, asking him if the map showed his route.

"No, it doesn't. You need Hole Hammer Road…and Yellow Springs Road," Autry replied, shrugging his shoulders. You could almost hear the jury's irritation.

I scribbled on the pad. "Should I go out and buy her a map to use?" Steve nodded and replied on the pad, "Don't think it'll help."

Thompson riffled through her papers, desperately trying to find Autry the correct map. She handed him exhibits and they were wrong. She handed him other exhibits, and they were hard to read. Autry was being deliberately obtuse, pretending to have no idea what she was asking and she was being accidentally obtuse, failing to understand his game. Their exchange started to sound a lot like the Abbott and Costello routine "Who's on First."

Thompson seemed to be the only one who didn't realize that Autry was making a fool of her. She handed Autry a photo depicting the area where Autry and Adams had planned to dump Holly's body. "Where in this area did you plan to dump the body?"

Autry squinted at the photo, muttering about how he couldn't see it. He finally glanced at the judge. "Your Honor, may I approach?"

There was laughter from the jury. The judge smiled, motioning for him to step forward. It was over for Thompson at that moment. The jury had taken Autry's side.

The trial finally ended with the jury convicting Zach Adams of the kidnapping, rape, and murder of Holly Bobo. I could feel the palpable relief from the Bobo family, and they hugged each other and those sitting near them. They ultimately left the courtroom, promising to have a press conference with the prosecutors in just a little while, asking the media to stay put.

It wasn't long before the family stood in front of the cameras, thanking the prosecutors and police for their hard work, and announcing that Zach Adams had agreed to plead guilty and that they did not want prosecutors to pursue the death penalty. Dylan Adams pleaded guilty and was sentenced to life in prison. Jason Autry's eight-year state prison sentence for solicitation of first-degree murder and facilitation of especially aggravated kidnapping ended on September 16, 2020, and he was released from prison.

However, on December 3, 2020, only three months after Autry's release from prison, a Benton County deputy observed Autry was arrested on gun possession charges. Prosecutors presented evidence in court that approximately twenty-five days after the beginning of his supervised release term, Autry was in possession of a Smith and Wesson, Model M&P shield and a nine-millimeter caliber pistol he had stolen. Within seventy-eight days of his release, he was also in possession of a Marlin, 30-30 caliber rifle as well as ammunition.

On November 22, 2022, Autry pled guilty to three counts of being a felon in possession of firearms and ammunition. At the sentencing hearing on June 24, 2024, the United States asked U.S. District Judge S. Thomas Anderson to apply an upward departure from Autry's guidelines range, arguing that Autry had an egregious criminal history that was not sufficiently reflected in that range. Judge Anderson agreed and sentenced Autry to 228 months in federal prison for the gun offenses.

The Sixth Circuit upheld the 228-month sentence, noting that Autry had a serious criminal past that included aggravated assault, drug trafficking, burglary, active membership in the violent Aryan Nation gang, and admitted participation in Bobo's abduction and murder. Furthermore, Autry had a reputation for violence in his community, was violent toward his romantic partners and family members, committed a racially motivated assault, and was involved in violent altercations and drug trafficking while serving prison sentences and during pre-trial detention.[12]

Following the trial, Dana and Karen Bobo moved to a new house and were finally able to bury and mourn Holly Bobo. Unfortunately, the Bobo case still wasn't over. In July 2024, a video of Jason Autry recanting his testimony about Holly Bobo's murder surfaced, setting the stage for Zach Adams's petition for a new trial. For Zach Adams's petition for a new trial to be successful, he had to prove that there was new evidence. Adams claimed that Autry met with a forensic neuropsychologist in December and admitted that he made the story up after his lawyer told him before the 2017 trial that Autry had a 95 percent chance of being convicted at trial. Autry claimed he decided to testify for the prosecution to avoid the death penalty and came up with the entire story while reviewing discovery evidence before the trial. Adams alleged that Autry used extensive cell phone data to create the story that he told the jury.

In September 2024, Tennessee Judge J. Brent Bradberry denied Adams's petition for a new trial, writing in his ruling,

[12] Sixth Circuit Court of Appeals Affirms 228-Month Sentence for Felon Convicted of Firearms Offenses, From Press Release by US Attorney's Office, Western District, TN

"Mr. Autry's new statements do not leave this court without serious or substantial doubt that Mr. Adams is innocent." However, in January 2025, Adams appealed Bradberry's ruling, claiming ineffective assistance of counsel, because Jennifer Thompson failed to introduce evidence of Adams's alibi. Adams claims that he was on his computer at the time of Holly Bobo's abduction. Additionally, Adams alleges that he, Dylan Adams, and Shane Austin went to the bank an hour later, at the time when Jason Autry testified that he and Adams were disposing of Holly Bobo's body. The state continues to maintain that Adams would have still been convicted, absent testimony from Jason Autry.

There has been no ruling on Adams's appeal as of May 2025.

CHAPTER FOUR

The Murder of Lula Young

I first heard about the Linda Leedom murder case in 1998, when my close friend Eric from New Orleans called to tell me that one of his oldest friends from Memphis was facing capital murder and conspiracy charges. Eric had gone to high school with Linda and described their friendship as extremely close. A mutual friend had just reached out with the shocking news: Linda might spend the rest of her life in prison.

By then, I'd already left the practice of law and was freelancing for magazines. I'd recently sold two crime stories to *Entertainment Weekly* and a few others to national outlets. I knew someone would want Linda's story.

Eric explained that Linda had started her career as a nurse before becoming a successful accountant with her own thriving business. She lived in Horn Lake, a small town in Mississippi, just across the Tennessee border. People in the area described her as respected, accomplished, and devoted to her husband, Gary, and their two grown children.

Her case would eventually land in Hernando, Mississippi, in the same courthouse where John Grisham tried his first case. A photo of Grisham still hangs in the lobby. The courthouse sits in a place called Courthouse Square—coincidentally, the same name Universal Studios gave its fictional town square in *Back to the Future.*

Eric wasn't entirely surprised by the charges. "She always had a rebellious streak," he told me. "Back in high school, Linda flaunted the rules." Unlike most of their classmates, she had her own car—a bright orange Mustang Mach 1. "We were all pretty poor back then, but not Linda," he said, the bitterness in his voice unmistakable. "When she ran out of money, she'd just ask her Daddy for more. She was always getting pulled over by police, making up stories about sick relatives, and talking her way out of tickets. She was good at talking her way out of trouble."

But this time, talking hadn't helped.

Linda was awaiting trial for the murder of her best friend, forty-seven-year-old Lula Young—a former EMT, a divorced mother of two, and, according to prosecutors, the target of a long con. The state alleged that after Lula's breast cancer diagnosis, Linda took out two life insurance policies in Lula's name, totaling $1 million, naming herself as beneficiary, even though Lula's adult children, Mike and Stacey, were still alive. A third policy, for $200,000, named Linda's husband, Gary, as the beneficiary.

During a search of the Leedom home, investigators discovered a partnership agreement between Linda and Lula and a power of attorney granting Linda control over Lula's affairs. Prosecutors also alleged that Linda enlisted her daughters—Melanie Leedom Wright and Jennifer Dodson—to help her illegally obtain the policies.

Linda's defense attorney, Bill Massey, countered that Lula had asked for help securing insurance so her children could have something after she died. Since Lula had already undergone a mastectomy and couldn't qualify for new insurance on her own, she allegedly asked Linda to find a way. Linda claimed she agreed to manage the money until Lula's children were off drugs. According to Massey, Linda always intended to give them the money when the time was right.

The Best of Friends

Lula Young married her husband, John, shortly after high school. They were both nineteen. John served in the navy's construction battalion and was stationed in Davisville, Rhode Island. He completed two tours in Vietnam, returning briefly between deployments. Though Lula mostly stayed in Mississippi, she did visit him between tours. When John left the navy, he returned to work in construction, taking jobs across Mississippi, Michigan, and Arkansas. In 1976, the couple settled in Mississippi and purchased the house where Lula would later pass away.

When I spoke with John, he recalled meeting Lula in high school.

"She was a nice-looking young woman," he said. "She was thin and had beautiful red hair, like her mother, Flora."

Their marriage, he said, was good for a long time—until life began to pull them in different directions.

"But then both of us changed—age, maturity," he told me. "Things primarily changed because I was gone a lot doing construction in different places. That was just the way I needed to make a living, and that's what I had to do to provide for my family," he added, still a little defensive. "I'd be away all week and then just come home on the weekends."

Lula and Linda became close friends after Lula and her family moved in next door to Linda's home in Mississippi. As young mothers, they bonded quickly, spending most of their time together and supporting each other through life's ups and downs. Although John Young was never particularly fond of Linda, he acknowledged that she and Lula got along well.

"Never cared much for her," he said. "She was a very overbearing person, dominating and controlling. I didn't like the way Linda treated her husband, Gary. I saw her knock Gary over a car hood with her fist. She was a pretty, good old gal with her hands."

John managed to work locally until about 1979, but after their children, Michael and Stacey, were born, he went back on the road. As his presence at home declined, Linda's friendship with Lula deepened. After Lula's divorce, Linda stepped in to help with the children, offering both emotional and occasional financial support. Lula began working as a nurse and later volunteered as a bookkeeper with the Horn Lake Fire Department, eventually earning her EMT license.

The women's friendship only strengthened when Lula was diagnosed with breast cancer in the late 1980s. Linda cared for her through chemo treatments, bought her groceries, and kept Lula's family—especially her mother, Flora—informed. Lula's relatives lived an hour away in Batesville and relied on Linda to provide updates.

"Linda was like a sister to Lula," Miss Flora recalled after her daughter's death. "Always there to help."

The treatments worked. After six years, Lula was declared cancer-free. But prosecutors would later argue that this was the moment her fate was sealed. According to young DA John Champion, Linda had been counting on Lula's death. And when it became clear her friend was going to live, she allegedly decided to kill her. But Linda didn't want to do it herself. Instead, she allegedly hired someone to do it for her—a decision that proved disastrous. Hitmen, it turns out, are often more loyal to plea deals than paychecks.

For years, investigators couldn't find anything to tie Linda to Lula's death. Then, in January 1997—four years after Lula died—authorities caught a break. An informant told DA investigator Chris Sheley that Charles Wayne Dunn had confessed to setting the fire. The friend claimed Dunn had said Linda approached him and asked how to kill Lula without getting caught. He agreed to wear a wire, but Dunn didn't take the bait.

Soon after, another informant emerged: a man who'd shared a jail cell with Dunn. He claimed Dunn had told him he'd been paid by Linda Leedom to kill Lula Young and that he'd been instructed to make it look like an accident so insurance would pay out. The informant stated that the confession occurred while the two were working together.

When Dunn was brought in for questioning, he was read his rights by Officer Randy Doss and DA investigator Sheley. Confronted with the informants' stories, he cracked. Dunn admitted that Linda had approached him, claiming Lula was terminally ill and suffering. She allegedly said that killing her would be an act of mercy. According to Dunn, she offered five thousand dollars for the job and told him to use a propane tank to start the fire.

Dunn said he visited Lula's home, gave her medication to make her sleep, and waited until she was unconscious before setting the fire. He claimed he opened a propane tank and placed paper on top of a heater, which ignited and caused the deadly blaze.

But it didn't stop there.

According to court records, Dunn had set another fire two years later, at Linda's daughter's home in Southaven. Investigators said Linda also collected insurance money from that fire. Dunn told them that he met Linda in late 1993, after she moved in with her daughter, Melanie Wright, and her son-in-law. He also said she gave him money to buy the heater he used to ignite the propane tank. The prosecution would later present a witness who claimed Linda had purchased a grill as a Christmas gift for her daughter and stored the grill and the propane tank at Lula's house.

Death by Fire

Lula was asleep in her home on December 19, 1994, when neighbors heard two explosions and then witnessed her home burst into flames. Mike Hancock, a member of the Horn Lake Volunteer Fire Department, was deputized as a county fire investigator and was working the fire scene for the Horn Lake Volunteer Fire Department. When Mike arrived on the scene, the fire was still burning. Although most people were told Lula died from smoke inhalation, her daughter would later inform me of the real circumstances of her death. Mike recalled seeing Linda arrive at the scene but remembered her being more worried about things in the house than what had happened to her friend.

"She asked me how the fire started," Mike told me in an interview. "I said I had no idea. And then she asked me if they were going to do an autopsy on the body, and if they did, was it going to show cancer? And, I told her, yeah, it's going to show that she had a radical mastectomy. It was pretty much common knowledge that Lula had one of her breasts removed. Linda's reaction to me was like, 'Do you know the coroner well enough that that could be left out of the report so her kids could get the insurance money?' I thought she was trying to get involved in insurance fraud for the sake of the kids."

Mike had known Lula Young for years. He had formerly lived next door to Lula Young, and he knew her well. Around 1989, Lula introduced him to Linda Leedom, who began doing his income taxes at around that time. Six or eight months before the fire, Mike and his wife, Jill, helped other neighbors in repairing and cleaning up the home occupied by Lula Young and her children, Stacey and Michael Young. He said that part of this cleanup included him installing smoke detectors in the living room and the hallway of the home. He also recalled that the smoke alarms he installed were First Alert units.

Mike explained that early on in the investigation at the fire scene, Chief Jerry Moore determined that he had a friendship with Lula Young and Linda Leedom and decided he should not be involved in the investigation. J.C. Smith, Mr. Mark Smith, and Mr. Wade Turner were tasked with doing the bulk of the investigation, with Mike observing. The investigators initially concluded that the fire had been started by faulty aluminum wiring. They also surmised, based on burn patterns, that the fire had started in a corner of the house. Two days later, Mike realized that they'd all been wrong about the cause of the fire. After having the chance to view photos taken by neighbors of Lula, Jan, and Junior Harris, before the fire trucks arrived, Mike realized that the team had come to the wrong conclusion. Based on Harris's photos, he was able to determine that they'd been wrong about a lot of things from seeing the way the structure was burning, the color of the flames, and the heaviest flame concentration. He also realized that the corner of the house they thought was where the electrical issue started was still completely intact at that point. What he'd seen during his investigation was that propane had run down the wall and gone into those corners.

"That's why we had burn patterns there that made it look electrical," Mike explained.

While on the scene, Mike saw David Krzyzkowski find the propane bottle. He witnessed David turn the valve on the bottle approximately one-quarter of a turn to determine if it was open or closed. The quarter turn was to close the bottle—it had been open. The bottle was lying on its side so that the propane would come out as a liquid. Mike recalled that the valve was pointed to the right of the front door. There were two or three oxygen bottles placed right near the front door.

The department decided to leave the cause of the fire as electrical, so Linda wouldn't know that the fire department knew that the propane tank was the cause. According to Mike, it was part of their effort to keep Linda in the dark because she had good sources not only in the fire department but also in the police department. When Linda had a fire in Southaven, Mississippi, where her daughter Jennifer Dobson lived, Mike called Chief White and told him that Linda had great sources. The chief claimed that he didn't have to worry about his people giving out information. Just a week later, Mike was talking to

Chief White and said he'd heard that an electrical engineer had been called out to the Southaven house to investigate. The chief told him that nobody was supposed to know that.

When I spoke with Lula's daughter, Stacey, in the summer of 1999, before Linda's trial, she said they'd told their grandmother that Lula had died in her bed after inhaling smoke, but the reality was much more gruesome. Lula's body was found on the floor of her bedroom, after she'd crawled to escape the flames engulfing her. It was the fumes that killed Lula. The coroner told Stacey that Lula probably took maybe one or two deep breaths, and that's what killed her. After years of chemotherapy and radiation, Lula's lungs weren't in the best shape. She was exposed to toxic fumes in the fire generated by the two explosions.

"I was standing there when the house blew up," Stacey said. "Two years after it happened, every time I close my eyes, I'd see the house explode. I saw them pull my mama out of her window and lay her down on the ground. The day after Mama died, I washed my hands so much. Every time I looked at my hands, they looked black. I could smell the smoke."

The police began their investigation into Lula's house fire in December 1994. They believed that Linda had something to do with the house fire that killed Lula Young. They didn't get a break in the case until 1997, when Charles Wayne Dunn confessed to a fellow inmate and police informant that he'd set the house fire that killed Lula Young. When questioned by two investigators from DeSoto County, Dunn claimed that Linda Leedom hired him to burn Lula Young in a house fire. The police ultimately executed a search warrant on Linda and Gary Leedom's home and found documentation of three life insurance policies for

Lula Young that listed Linda Leedom or a family member as a beneficiary.

Police also discovered that after her death, Linda went about the business of collecting payments on Lula's various life insurance policies. She'd taken out almost $1 million worth of life insurance with herself, her husband, and her daughter as the beneficiaries. In each of those policies, Linda had falsely claimed to be Lula Young's sister. There was a required physical examination that was conducted, and Linda was the one who underwent the examination. Linda was the person who signed all three of those policies. Two of them ended up paying off after Lula's murder, with Linda collecting $75,000 on one as well as $200,000 on the other. Leedom's claim on the $500,000 life insurance policy she had taken out from Nationwide Insurance was denied.

In the fall of 1997, two years before her murder trial, Linda Leedom was charged with two felonies of insurance and mail fraud and pleaded guilty to one count of wire fraud and two counts of mail fraud in U.S. Federal Court in Aberdeen, Mississippi. She was sentenced to twenty-seven months in prison, followed by three years of supervised release, and was ordered to pay $275,000 in restitution to the insurance companies she had defrauded. Her daughter, Jennifer Leedom Dodson, also pleaded guilty to her part in the insurance fraud. She was sentenced to three years in prison, along with a fine. In March of 1997, Linda Leedom was indicted on murder and arson charges.

The Other Victim

Lula Young wasn't the only person Linda Leedom targeted. After Lula's death, Linda set her sights on another vulnerable victim:

Robert Stovall, a mentally challenged handyman who occasionally worked for her.

According to Charles Wayne Dunn, Linda contacted him again after Lula's murder. This time, she introduced him to Stovall and offered him ten thousand dollars—double what he was paid to kill Lula—to murder the unsuspecting handyman. Dunn said Linda never gave him a reason for wanting Stovall dead. But, as with Lula, she had already taken out life insurance policies on him—totaling $200,000—and named herself the sole beneficiary.

Dunn agreed to the plan and began laying the groundwork. He obtained a fraudulent ID card bearing his own photo but listing Robert Stovall's name. Linda paid for the fake ID and also financed the purchase of a Toyota Celica. The plan was to stage a deadly car crash that would kill Stovall. Dunn would pose as Stovall, and the crash would appear accidental—just as the fire had with Lula.

Leedom even traveled with Dunn to Selmer, Tennessee, where Stovall lived. There, she instructed him to purchase the Celica, which he would later use in the staged collision. Fortunately for Stovall, Linda was arrested before the plan could be executed.

When detectives searched Leedom's home, they uncovered critical evidence. Among the documents was a driver's license with Dunn's photo, but the name on the ID was Robert Stovall. Investigators also found the life insurance policies Linda had taken out on Stovall's life. Robert had no knowledge that such policies existed, nor that he'd come perilously close to becoming Linda's next victim.

On August 31, 1999, following a one-week trial, a jury found Linda Leedom guilty of capital murder and conspiracy to commit capital murder. She was sentenced to life in prison without the possibility of parole, plus an additional twenty years.

Her husband, Gary Leedom, struck a deal with prosecutors for his role in signing insurance checks. He received a $250 fine and a one-hundred-dollar assessment to the United States Crime Victims Fund and was ordered to pay court costs. After thirty-six months, Gary's case was dismissed—leaving him free to continue his life without a felony conviction.

CHAPTER FIVE

The Investigation Begins

I finally managed to make the trip from Los Angeles to Memphis, just a few weeks before the start of Linda Leedom's trial. Since speaking with my friend about the trial, I'd done a great deal of research about Linda Leedom's insurance fraud scheme that had ended with her pleading guilty. I was reluctantly impressed with her scheme of posing as Lula, especially since it had almost succeeded. She'd seemed a smarter-than-average criminal, until I began reading in the Memphis paper, *The Commercial Appeal*, about her alleged role in the murder of Lula Young. The story was complicated and I spoke to the prosecutor, the defense attorney, and even briefly with some fire investigators, before I ever left Los Angeles. My most interesting discovery about Linda Leedom actually came during my call with the reporter from *The Commercial Appeal*, who explained that Linda Leedom was well-liked in her community, and that most of her neighbors liked and trusted her, including those in law enforcement and in the volunteer fire department for Horn Lake. After years of caring for Lula Young, while Young went through chemotherapy and had a breast removed, Linda had earned a reputation among her and Lula's friends as kind and selfless. She didn't really fit the profile of a woman committed to killing her best friend for $1 million in insurance proceeds.

It was raining when my plane from Los Angeles landed in Memphis. Dark skies, thick humidity, and a hard, unrelenting downpour—it was perfect weather for a murder trial. I pressed my face against the tiny window, trying to catch a glimpse of the landscape through the sheets of rain. A loud crack of thunder startled the man beside me awake; he'd slept through the entire flight.

The drive from the airport to my hotel was filled with excitement. The rain landed on the car in sheets, exposing my inexperience at driving in the rain to anyone who had the misfortune to be behind me. I'd booked a room at the Hollywood Hotel and Casino in Tunica, Mississippi, which allowed me to not only view some Elvis memorabilia but also to make use of the casino after being in court all day. The trial was taking place in Hernando, Mississippi, because Horn Lake, where the murder occurred, didn't have a courthouse. Hernando was around thirty minutes south of Memphis. With a population of just eight thousand, Hernando was so small and isolated that you had to fly into another state just to get there.

Driving along the Mississippi River, following vague directions from the rental agency, I thought again about my call with Bill Bayne, the veteran crime reporter at *The Commercial Appeal* in Memphis. Bill had covered murder trials across Tennessee and northern Mississippi for more than fifteen years. He'd given me a good sense of what to expect at Linda's trial.

I asked who he expected to take the stand and how long the trial might last.

"I expect that the state's main witness will be Charles Wayne Dunn, who's going to testify about how Linda Leedom hired him to kill good ole Lula. That guy was the hitman in all this. But I can't imagine the whole trial will take more than a week."

"For a murder trial?" I asked incredulously.

I'd never followed a capital murder trial that wrapped in just a week. Linda wasn't just accused of killing one person—she'd also been planning to kill another.

"It's not going to last eight months like the O.J. Simpson one. This isn't Los Angeles," he said with a chuckle. "Miss Leedom is about to find out that there's nothing quite like the iron fist of Mississippi justice. They aren't known for acquitting murderers down here."

I laughed politely but didn't take the bait. There'd be time enough to discuss O.J. during the Leedom trial. I had a feeling Bill and I would become friends. He seemed like the kind of guy who'd help me navigate the courthouse crowd and introduce me to the locals.

When I asked who I should talk to first, Bill didn't hesitate.

"You need to talk to the DA's chief investigator, Chris Sheley. He's the reason that Linda Leedom is sitting in prison today. If Chris hadn't come along, Robert Stovall would be dead and Linda would be free—spending that insurance money and planning her next murder."

I brought up the defense's argument: that Lula Young had asked Linda to take out the insurance policies for her children. Given her mastectomy, Lula likely wouldn't have qualified for insurance on her own. It wasn't inconceivable that she'd ask a friend for help.

"Don't believe it," Bill replied. "Lula wouldn't have been part of any insurance fraud. Linda killed her best friend, plain and simple. When they were in court last time, I looked over at them, and Linda was sitting there with her husband, Gary, looking all happy and smiling. She was talking with her attorney, laughing, and it was like all of them were at a party or something."

I asked whether he thought Gary had been involved in the murder plot.

"Nah. Linda told him to sign some forms, and he did. When Gary isn't out in his truck driving around, he's home watching television. He's not quite right in the head, if you know what I mean."

"Is he mentally handicapped?" I asked.

"No, he's retarded. He had a stroke a few years back, and his brain just doesn't work right anymore." He paused. "Gary didn't have anything to do with murdering Lula—but them two girls of his did. The police believe they both knew about the murder. The younger one, Melanie, was sleeping with the guy who burned down Lula's house."

"The hitman? Charles Wayne Dunn?"

"That's the one. I asked around, and everyone knew about the affair. It's a small town, Horn Lake."

I asked Bill why he believed Dunn. The guy was an addict and his story wasn't exactly consistent. Couldn't he be lying to save himself from the death penalty?

"Sure, but I think he's telling the truth. No way Linda Leedom would do her own dirty work. If you want to get the full story, you need to talk to Lula's mother, Miss Flora. She was shocked when she found out that Linda was the one who killed Lula because she was always really close with Linda. You know Linda was the one who nursed Lula through her breast cancer. Miss Flora knows a lot about that family."

"Linda seemed to be a good friend for a while."

"Right up until she decided to burn her up alive. The whole thing is unbelievable. When Lula first got sick with cancer, Linda even drove her down to Grenada for a family reunion. Even after Lula died, Linda stayed tight with the Young folks. She was over at the house right before the funeral, helping make all the arrangements. Lula's whole family is still in shock. They're nice people too. When you get to the courthouse, make sure you go over and introduce yourself. They plan on being there every day, along with their brother Bobby."

Bill explained that Lula's family lived in Grenada, Mississippi, about one hundred miles south of Horn Lake. They hadn't been able to visit often while Lula was undergoing chemo, and they'd come to rely on Linda to care for her.

"Like I said before, she's a cold one," he added. "Just ask Lula's sister Margaret about her. She said that during the viewing, Linda looked Miss Flora in the eye and just started bawling about how much she was going to miss Lula. Crazy stuff."

The Fire

After forty minutes on the road, I spotted the hotel. A dazzling green billboard emerged from the darkness of cotton fields and marshland: *Welcome to Fitzgerald's Hotel and Casino.* Promising all the luck of the Irish, Fitzgerald's offered everything from majestic castle-style rooms to a chance to kiss a genuine piece of the Blarney Stone. Bally's Casino Tunica leaned into local flavor, offering a nostalgic return to the Mississippi Delta of the 1800s and a modern, twenty-four-hour all-you-can-eat buffet. I opted for the Hollywood Hotel and Casino—Tinseltown magic in the heart of Tunica.

The next morning, I called Chris Sheley. We agreed to meet near the courthouse in Horn Lake around 11:00 a.m. I expected the usual: a buttoned-up lawman with a chip on his shoulder about journalists. But Chris surprised me. Yes, he was committed to the job. But he didn't take himself too seriously. I liked him right away.

It might've been the Southern charm or the dry humor, or just how willing he was to talk about the case. He was warm, engaging, and unexpectedly opinionated. (He referred to HBO as "Hell's Box Office," the first time I'd heard that take.) Chris had the cynicism of a veteran cop but also a sincere, boots-on-the-ground sense of justice. He'd worked for years to gather enough evidence to charge Linda Leedom.

We ended up having lunch at a local Chinese restaurant. I was skeptical about eating Chinese food in Mississippi, but I managed to survive it with only minimal gastrointestinal distress. After that, I stuck to barbecue.

Chris told me he'd grown up in Panola County, served four and a half years in the army stationed in Hawaii, earned a degree in accounting from the University of Mississippi, and trained at the FBI Academy in Quantico. After years in the Horn Lake Police Department, he joined the DA's office in 1996. He and Police Chief Sammy Webb were the ones who ultimately uncovered that Linda Leedom had murdered Lula Young.

On the morning of the fire, Chris was among the first officers on scene. He didn't know Linda well—they'd met once over a rental dispute involving one of her tenants. But he remembered her behavior that morning.

"I remember that she was in a housecoat and running around [like] a chicken with her head cut off," he said, mid-bite of an egg roll. "I hadn't yet joined the district attorney's office. I didn't know Linda well, but I sure got to know her during the investigation."

I asked what people in Horn Lake thought of her. "Was she well-liked?"

"Yeah, you could say that. She did the taxes for most of the firefighters, police, and other folks in the area and was pretty well-liked. I think, given who she was in the community, we wouldn't have looked her way after the fire if she hadn't tried to point us to Lula's ex-husband."

Chris recounted a telling detail from a witness that morning.

"One of her friends who was there at the fire told me that when she saw Linda, she was smoking a cigarette and swearing. She said, 'That son of a bitch. I know he did this.' Linda was acting angry, and in the same breath, she told the witness that the fire was her fault."

But there was another statement—an inadvertent confession—that raised alarm.

"Linda's exact words were 'I feel like it's my fault. You know I had that gas grill hidden in Michael's bedroom for Christmas.' I mean, she admitted she'd put the propane tank in Lula's house. She claimed it was a gift for Gary that she was hiding at Lula's. Once we figured out that the fire was arson, we looked at her."

I said, "So, she was, in essence, the architect of her own demise."

"You could put it that way," Chris replied with a laugh.

Even before the fire, Lula's house wasn't much to look at. A modest 1970s ranch, 1,200 square feet, three bedrooms, a bath, and a kitchen—one of several identical homes squeezed into a cul-de-sac. The fire erupted just before 6:00 a.m. on a cold December morning.

Fourteen-year-old Brian Riles was jolted awake by a loud explosion.

"When I walked on over to the window, I saw flames shooting out of Miss Lula's roof," Brian told police. "I watched for a second until I realized that Miss Lula and her daughter, Stacey, might be trapped in there. That's when I grabbed my sweatpants and my sneakers and went running to get my dad."

Bonito Motto, a rookie dispatcher, was near the end of his shift when the fire broke out.

"I was just lying back getting ready for my shift to end, and at about 5:55 a.m., the phone just started ringing off the hook," Bonito told me. "I toned out Engine One and let them know we had a fully involved residential fire at 6875 Northwood Cove and that there'd been reports of explosions and hissing sounds coming from the home. I handled at least fourteen calls about the fire that morning. I think everyone in town saw the blaze."

Firefighter Mike Casey, who'd known Lula from her EMT days, was among the first on scene.

"By the time we arrived on the scene, the fire had already destroyed nearly 60 percent of the house," he wrote in his report. "I immediately prepared to go in through the back window into Miss Young's bedroom to start a primary search."

But entering wasn't easy. The headboard of Lula's waterbed blocked the window. Casey had to crawl over it. There, at the foot of the bed, he found Lula's body—face down, severely burned.

With sheetrock falling and flames closing in, Casey and two other firefighters struggled to lift Lula's 230-pound frame onto a stretcher and hoist it out the window. But it was too late. Lula was already dead.

Deputy Chief Jerry Moore, one of the first on scene, knew right away something was off.

"When I pulled up, the whole front of the house was gone—the front door and the two front windows. Fire was lapping over the roof, and the door area was just a solid inferno.... You don't see them burn very often like that without some type of assistance. At that point, I wasn't saying somebody set this fire. I just knew that something was wrong."

They focused efforts on rescue rather than suppression, Moore said, just enough to preserve Lula's body for an open-casket funeral. While crews cleared smoldering debris, Lula's son-in-law approached Moore.

"I was standing at the front and [Steve] just walked up and said, 'There is a full propane bottle in the front bedroom of the house,'" Moore recalled. They found the tank, valve partially open, lying on its side—the exact conditions needed for a liquid-fueled inferno. Later that day, Linda Leedom approached Mike Hancock, a fire investigator. She asked about the fire's origin, then something far more troubling.

"She then asked if I knew him well enough, where the part about the mastectomy would be left out of his report so that Lula's kids could get the insurance money."

Hancock refused. At the time, he'd written the fire off as an electrical incident. But photographs taken by neighbors made him reconsider. The burn patterns didn't align with the electrical wiring. Propane had spread throughout the house.

Craig Burnett, a former tenant of Linda's, also had a story to tell. She'd once made him work off back rent by mowing six acres. He described her as charming, educated, and calculating.

"She was very personable and outgoing…but she was also a greedy person." He remembered seeing her the morning of the fire. "She came running up to me with an old-style hard makeup case. She told me that it was all Lula's medication and that she didn't want Buckethead to get hold of it."

Buckethead was Lula's son, Michael. Linda was already shaping the narrative, portraying Lula's kids as drug addicts, and herself as the responsible protector.

The next day, a confidential informant contacted Moore. Someone had taken out excessive life insurance on Lula Young. Investigators met to reevaluate the case. Everyone suspected arson. And Linda.

Linda began calling Hancock, asking to meet in person. He agreed—and wore a wire.

"She tells me some guy who she'd hired is trying to blackmail her and is asking for money or he'll go to the police and say she set the fire…. She finally got angry and said, 'Do I need a lawyer?' I told her she only needed one if she was guilty. Innocent people don't need lawyers, only guilty ones."

By January, investigators were convinced the fire wasn't accidental. The physical evidence was thin, but the circumstantial case against Linda Leedom was growing stronger by the day.

The Hitman

Over lunch, Chris Sheley told me about the man at the center of the murder plot: Charles Wayne Dunn. Dunn, Chris believed, was the missing link—the hired hand who made it possible to arrest Linda Leedom for the murder of Lula Young.

The breakthrough occurred on February 3, 1997, when investigator Aubrey Broadway contacted Chris regarding an informant at the DeSoto County Jail. The man, David Vincent, claimed he had information about an old house fire in Horn Lake. Chris's interest was immediate. He had long suspected that Leedom had an alibi for the night of the fire because she'd hired someone to do her dirty work.

Chris met Broadway that day, and the two headed to the jail to speak with Vincent. Inside the interrogation room, Vincent described a man named Wayne Dunn, who had done landscaping at his house two years earlier. During their conversations, Dunn grew despondent and admitted he'd killed an older woman—but claimed she was already dying.

"Dunn admitted that his employer had paid him to kill this older lady," Vincent said. "She told him that Lula had about ten thousand dollars' worth of insurance that would just barely cover funeral services and expenses and stuff. And she told him about all the pain and suffering that the woman was going through."

When Vincent asked how the woman was killed, Dunn said he'd burned her house down, disguising the blaze to look like an accident. He added that he'd drugged her heavily so she wouldn't feel pain when the fire started.

"Dunn was boasting about his intelligence," Chris said with a wry smile. "Always good when the dumb ones think they're smart."

According to Vincent, Dunn also revealed that he was working for Melanie's mother, painting houses and doing odd jobs. While he couldn't recall the names of the mother or daughter, he remembered that Melanie lived on Carroll Cove and her parents lived on Church Road—the addresses matched the Leedom's.

"Do you think Dunn confessed because he felt guilty?" I asked.

"Probably not about the guilt," Chris replied. "He admitted the people who paid him were family to Melanie. He'd been burning a Ford for her for the insurance money. Got paid a few hundred a week in cash."

Chris then pulled Dunn's file. The man had a felony record in DeSoto County and was still on probation. On his forms, Dunn had listed Linda Leedom as both his employer and a contact.

Chris devised a plan. He worked with Dunn's probation officer to bring him in—along with Vincent—under the pretense of updating paperwork. Vincent arrived first and was wired for sound. Chris gave him specific instructions: mention Lula Young by name and ask if Dunn ever got over what he'd done.

Once both men were in the room, Vincent asked about "that thing that had been bothering" Dunn. Dunn admitted he still felt guilty about killing the woman in Horn Lake but reassured Vincent that "no one had ever figured out it was arson." He believed he'd gotten away with it. Chris decided it was time. He entered the room and confronted Dunn.

"I told him we knew he'd done something he regretted while smoking crack, that he'd been paid to kill someone, and that it still haunted him," Chris said. Dunn was read his rights and arrested.

Then he began to talk.

He confessed to being paid five thousand dollars by Linda Leedom to kill Lula Young. Linda had told him that Lula had cancer and was going to die anyway, and that killing her would be "doing her a favor." Dunn described how he set the fire: by placing a heater by a chair near the front door, stuffing newspapers in front of it, and walking away.

Chris now had enough to arrest Leedom, but he wanted more. On February 2, 1997, Chris convinced Dunn to wear a wire and visit Linda at her home on Church Road. A few days later, he handed me a transcript of their conversation.

Dunn: "It's been on my mind a lot."

Linda: "Has it? Well, honey, you can't let that bother you.... But what in the hell are you thinking about Lula?"

Dunn: "That shit just bothers me. I'll get over it one day."

Linda: "You've got to put it in the back of your mind and get on with it. Because I don't care what anybody says, I think she's better off."

Dunn: "I come over here to see if I can borrow some money to go to Oregon so I can get away. I've got to get away."

Linda: "Bless your heart."

Linda agreed to give him two hundred dollars a few days later. She never explicitly admitted to anything incriminating, but it was clear she wanted Dunn gone. She knew he was close to talking.

After the visit, Dunn returned to the probation office and offered more details. He told the complete story of what happened before Lula died in the fire he'd set. On the night before the fire, Dunn parked his car in Young's driveway and entered the house. He retrieved the heater from his truck, crushed some newspaper nearby, opened the valve on the propane tank, turned on the heater, and left the house. He testified the next day he went to Leedom's home and collected one thousand dollars from her with the balance to be paid in smaller amounts over time.[13]

His confession to using the propane tank to start the fire corroborated what fire investigators had found at the scene. He also confessed to setting another fire for Linda: the house belonging to her daughter, Jennifer Dodson, in Southaven. He said Linda had collected insurance money from that fire too.

To corroborate Dunn's claims, investigators spoke with his roommate, Jack Emmons. Emmons confirmed Dunn's story, saying Dunn had confessed to killing Lula Young. Dunn had even approached Emmons with another job: he offered him one thousand dollars to help kill a man in Selmer, Tennessee.

Emmons declined.

The documents seized from Linda Leedom's house were also very helpful to the investigation into not only insurance fraud, but also into the fire at Lula's home.

Police recovered the following incriminating documents:

- Three signed insurance policies written under Lula Young's name
- An ID card for Robert A. Stovall, bearing Charles Dunn's photo
- A Blue Cross Team Care card for Robert Stovall
- A credit application in the names of Melanie Wright and Robert Stovall for a 1995 Nissan pickup
- A credit life insurance policy naming Melanie Wright and Robert Stovall as the insured

13 "Linda Leedom v. State of Mississippi." 2025. Justia Law. https://law.justia.com/cases/mississippi/supreme-court/2001/conv10936.html.

It turned out that Robert Stovall was a mentally disabled man from Selmer, Tennessee. According to ADA John Champion, Melanie Wright said he had been targeted for another insurance scheme. If investigators hadn't intervened, Stovall might have suffered the same fate as Lula Young.

The plan to kill Lula, it seemed from both witness interviews and documents, had been in motion for a lot longer than investigators had initially believed. Linda had taken out a $500,000 double indemnity policy with Nationwide Insurance. It included a $200,000 accidental death benefit. But in September 1994, Lula began chemotherapy, and her health took a turn for the worse. Linda delayed the murder—convinced that Lula might die on her own.

Then, in December 1994, Lula went to the doctor for a follow-up.

"She got good news from her doctor," Chris told me. "I think that when Lula told Linda about the prognosis, Linda decided to go forward with the plan. Lula had survived cancer. But she wouldn't survive Linda."

The Funeral

After spending days interviewing police officers and fire investigators, I turned my attention to the people who knew Lula Young best—her family. I wanted to understand when, if ever, they began to suspect that Linda Leedom, Lula's best friend, might have been involved in her death.

It wasn't easy for Lula's family to speak ill of Linda. She had been right there in the aftermath—helping to plan the funeral, comforting Lula's mother, Miss Flora, and talking with her sisters. Linda had been a constant presence during Lula's darkest moments: through her divorce, chemotherapy, and struggles with her children's addiction.

The obituary told only part of the story:

"Lula Welch Young, 47, of Horn Lake, Miss., transcriber, died Monday of smoke inhalation in her home.... She was a volunteer EMT with the Horn Lake Volunteer Fire Department. Services will be held at 10:30 AM at Leflore Baptist Church with burial at the church cemetery."

The church was located in Grenada, Mississippi, near where Lula's extended family still lived.

The obituary continued:

"Mrs. Young leaves a daughter, Stacey Long, a son, Michael Long, both of Horn Lake; her mother, Flora Welch; two sisters, Nettie Minyard and Margaret Ward; and two brothers, Bobby Welch and Randy Welch, all of Holcomb, Mississippi."

Before the trial began, I arranged to meet Lula's family. We chose a Cracker Barrel in Bates, Mississippi—a midpoint between Horn Lake and their home in Holcomb. I asked about the funeral. I'd heard through firefighter Mike Hancock that it'd been a difficult event. Lula's sister Margaret was the first to speak.

"We wanted to have an open-casket funeral," Margaret told me. "I was looking at her hands at the funeral parlor, and they told us that they might not be able to keep the casket open for more than an hour at a time. I got to look at her, and she was wearing a necklace with a cross that I'd bought her for Christmas.... She'd had it on the night of the fire, and it had burned down into her neck."

The funeral home staff suggested a turban to cover Lula's head.

"She hated wigs," Margaret said. "She said they were itchy and wouldn't wear them when she was going through chemotherapy.... She ended up looking well...the eyelashes and the eyebrows were singed off, and some of the skin had peeled, but she looked extremely well to have been through what she had in the fire. The folks at the funeral home did a wonderful job."

I asked if Linda's behavior had seemed off during the service.

"She came in wearing a blue dress with her husband," Margaret recalled. "When Lula's obituary ran that morning, Linda got upset that we hadn't listed her as one of Lula's sisters.

"She believed that she was closer to Lula than we were, her actual sisters," she added, clearly still bitter. "We just laughed it off, but I think she was trying to show us how close they were to throw off any suspicion.... How could Linda ever kill Lula when she was so close with all of us?"

Lula's sister, Nettie Minyard, admitted she had been taken in by Linda's helpfulness.

"When Lula got sick, Linda sent over a lady to clean up the place. Remember Margaret," she said, glancing at her sister, "how we thought Linda was so nice for taking care of Lula like that? She was always over there.... We couldn't be up there with Lula all the time.... We went up there when we could, but we were all so busy with work and the kids."

At the funeral, Linda's only odd moment—besides the obituary—was how she handled Stacey and Mike, Lula's children.

According to Nettie, "When we were all standing out there on the porch, Stacey and Mike got to talking about how Lula died.... Stacey started describing how, when she closed her eyes, she kept seeing Lula's house explode over and over again...she couldn't get the image of Lula's coffin being put into the ground and dreamed about her mother trying to crawl out of there."

Margaret shook her head.

"She didn't like Lula's kids," she said. "Even at the funeral, she turned to me and said she loved my sister, but I had to admit she had the two most idiotic kids in the whole universe. She said those two put the 'func' in dysfunction."

When Stacey and Mike began talking, Linda marched over and told them to "hush up" so their grandmother wouldn't hear.

"She told them, 'If anyone asks, Lula died a peaceful death in her sleep,'" Margaret added.

Later, Stacey and her husband Steve approached Linda and asked for money.

"Steve complained that Stacey's clothes had burned in the fire," Margaret said. "Linda let her have it. She told her that Lula had kicked her out of the house three days before she died. 'You didn't lose anything. Most of your things were over in Nesbit.'"

Steve got angry, arguing that the insurance money belonged to Stacey.

"Don't you be telling me what Lula would have wanted. Not now, not ever," Linda had snapped back.

It wasn't until Linda's arrest that the family began to suspect anything.

"It all kind of still feels make-believe," Nettie said, rubbing her eyes. "We all can't believe she did this to Lula. It's been hardest on Mama. She thought of Linda like a daughter."

Miss Flora had trusted Linda implicitly. After Lula's death, Linda even sent her a check for two thousand dollars, made payable to the church in remembrance of Lula, and three hundred dollars for a tombstone. Both checks came from the Estate of Lula Young—meaning Lula had unknowingly paid for her own memorial.

"In January of 1997, Linda sent her a three-hundred-dollar check with instructions not to tell Lula's children," Margaret said. "She wrote a note: 'Happy gas bill payment.'"

Investigators asked Miss Flora if Linda had given her any of Lula's personal belongings. She said Linda had offered Lula's wheelchair, but she declined it, wondering, silently, why it hadn't burned in the fire.

Linda also gave her Lula's medicine bag, some jewelry, and her purse.

Miss Flora had only been aware of two small life insurance policies Lula held: a $25,000 policy from Baptist Hospital and a two-thousand-dollar credit union policy. She had no idea about the larger, fraudulent policies until federal investigators contacted her.

What Lula's family thought had been a painful accident was slowly being revealed as a betrayal too deep to fathom. And the woman who had stood with them at the casket, grieving beside them, had orchestrated it all.

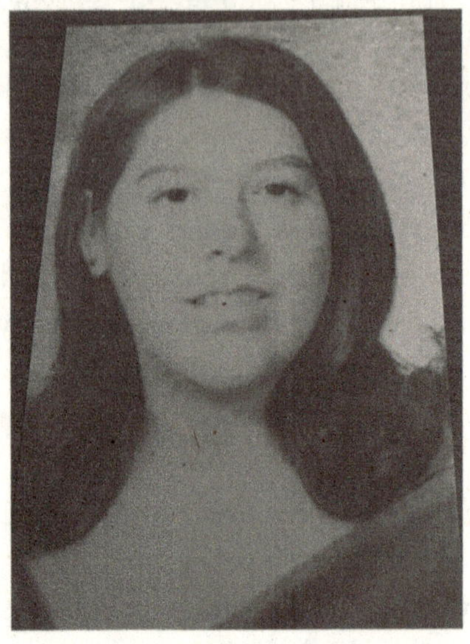

Photo of Linda Leedom from high school courtesy of Eric Whitmeyer and AG investigator Chris Sheley.

Detective Aubrey Broadway.

Lula Young in the hospital with cancer with her grandson from December 8th. She died on the 19th. (Courtesy of Lula's sister, Margaret Young.)

Judge Andrew Baker who presided over Linda Leedom's murder trial in the DeSoto County Courthouse.

Assistant DA John Champion and DA Bobby Williams. (Both have passed.)

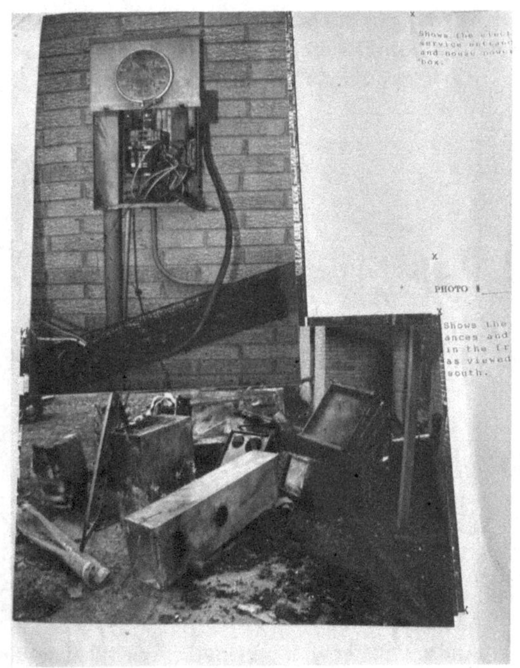

Electrical panel in Lula Young's home post-fire.

Lula Young's burned living room following fire set by hit man, Wayne Dunn.

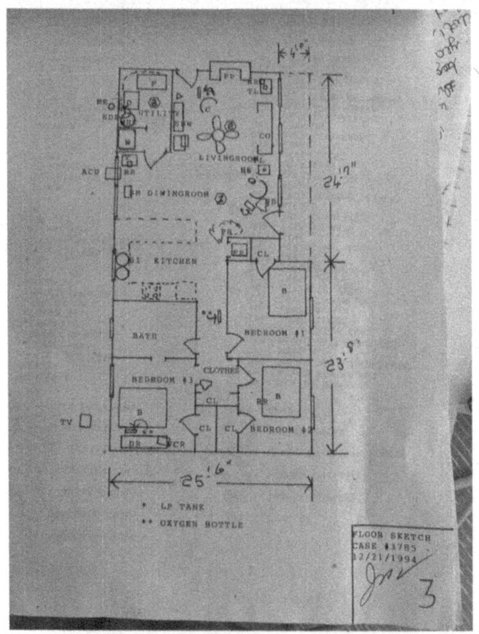

The layout of Lula Young's home as drawn by the fire department.

Heater used to set fire to Lula Young's house.

DA investigator, Chris Sheley.

Photo taken at Young Family reunion in 1993.
(Courtesy of Lula's sister, Margaret Young.)

Photo taken at Lula's Birthday Party in October 1993.

Photo of Margaret Ward, Lula's sister who provided me with photos of the family with her other sister, Nettie Maynard.

CHAPTER SIX

With Friends Like Linda

The road from Tunica to Hernando ended in front of the courthouse—a two-story red brick building with three imposing white columns. It looked like it had been built by central casting: a brick facade, white pillars, an expansive green lawn, and shady oaks. About fifteen people stood on the courthouse steps, chatting and smoking, waiting for court to begin. I walked inside and introduced myself to the clerk.

"This courthouse is a Mississippi state landmark," she said, pointing toward the front doors. "Make sure you take a look at the picture of John Grisham. He tried his first case here. And yes, he won."

Linda's trial was quick and dirty.

The courtroom was only partially full. Linda's defense lawyer, Bill Massey, was a respected Memphis criminal defense attorney with a long track record in high-profile cases. When I interviewed him beforehand, he said Linda planned to argue she committed insurance fraud at Lula's urging. According to Massey, Lula had wanted to leave money for her children but knew she'd never qualify for life insurance because of her cancer.

Bill Bayne, the local reporter, watched Massey warily.

"Folks around here don't like outsiders telling them how to do things," Bayne muttered. "His haircut costs more than I make in a year. He just got a guy off a triple homicide in Memphis, but he's not going to convince a Mississippi jury that Linda Leedom is innocent. This isn't LA."

The bailiff opened the door and led in Linda Leedom. Her husband, Gary, a thin man with gray hair clinging to a bald head, stood behind the defense table, waving weakly. Linda waved back with a wide smile. Gary rushed forward to hug her before the bailiff directed him to his seat. Behind him sat Linda's mother, an older woman with a hacking cough.

Linda chatted with her attorneys and scribbled on a yellow legal pad. She fit the role of the murderous best friend: thick seventies-style glasses, greasy gray ponytail, fifty extra pounds on her five-foot-seven frame, and an ill-fitting black skirt. She smiled and whispered with her lawyer.

When the Honorable Judge Andrew Baker entered, everyone stood. He had the standard look: gray hair, oversized glasses, and a stern expression.

"You may be seated," he said coolly as he riffled through papers. After reminding the gallery about courtroom decorum, he announced that the trial would be delayed to resolve procedural issues and summoned the attorneys into his chambers.

By the start of Linda Leedom's murder trial, the following indictments, plea deals and other court proceedings had occurred. In 1996, Leedom, along with her daughter, Jennifer Dotson, was indicted in 1996 in federal court on charges that she conspired with Dotson to fraudulently acquire life insurance policies on the life of Linda's best friend, Lula Young. Before going to trial on the federal charges, Linda Leedom was indicted on March 11, 1997, on charges of capital murder, conspiracy to commit murder, arson, and conspiracy to commit arson. In January, Leedom pleaded guilty to three counts of mail fraud, while her daughter Jennifer also pleaded guilty for her part in the insurance scam.

In addition to having already been charged federally and pleaded guilty, Jennifer Leedom Dotson was also charged in state court in 1997 with two counts of conspiracy to commit false pretenses. Jennifer's sister, Melanie Wright, was also charged with the same two counts. The court sentenced Jennifer Dotson to a term of two years in the Mississippi State Department of Corrections and permitted the sentence to run concurrently with her federal sentence, 2:96CR136-D-B, a sentence from the Northern District of Mississippi which began on March 2, 1998. At the time of her sentencing in September 1999, Jennifer Dotson had five months remaining on her federal sentence. Melanie Wright also pleaded guilty to conspiracy to commit false pretense and was sentenced to serve two years in the custody of the Mississippi Department of Corrections, but she was instead placed on the Intensive Supervision Program/House Arrest Program to do her time.

The state opened with a statement from Prosecutor John Champion, who introduced DA investigator Chris Sheley at the prosecution table.

Champion laid out the state's case: Linda had taken out $975,000 in life insurance on Lula, falsely claiming to be her sister.

"The interesting thing," Champion told the jury, "is that Lula Young was not insurable. She had a radical mastectomy in 1990."

He explained that a person must have an insurable interest to take out a life insurance policy on someone else. Friendship didn't count. Insurance agents would testify that they never met Lula. The only person they met was Linda.

Champion told the jury that Linda had bought a propane tank and floor heater and stored them at Lula's house. He previewed the testimony of Charles Wayne Dunn, the hitman who said Linda paid him five thousand dollars to kill Lula.

"Linda told Wayne that Lula wanted this done—that she wanted to be put out of her misery," Champion said. He added that Linda instructed Dunn to make the fire look like an accident.

Dunn bought a floor heater from the Target on Elvis Presley Boulevard. He placed newspaper on top of the heater, turned it on, and the propane tank ignited a flash fire.

Bill Massey began his opening by attacking Dunn's credibility: "They told you Dunn was an arsonist who burned Linda Leedom's best friend alive. What they didn't tell you is that he's also a crack cocaine addict who had a crush on Linda's daughter, Melanie."

Massey insisted Linda truly loved Lula.

"It was Linda who took her to the doctor, picked up her medicines, cared for her daily."

The two had concocted an insurance scheme to benefit Lula's children, Massey said. Lula trusted Linda to invest the money and help her kids.

The prosecution moved fast. First came Lula's sister, Margaret Ward. She testified they were close and spoke often. Lula had told her, "I don't know whether I have a tomorrow with cancer."

Margaret confirmed that Linda and Lula were frequently together and that Linda had been very helpful.

Then came the firefighters. Lt. Mike Casey described how he arrived to find Lula's house engulfed. He entered through a bedroom window and found Lula prone at the foot of her bed. He and Lt. York used a backboard to get her out while pushing back flames with a hose.

"When we got out," Casey said, "I told them to squirt me down. My back felt like it was on fire." He sat in the yard afterward, collecting his thoughts.

Lt. York testified that he didn't see the propane tank until after the fire was extinguished. He noted multiple oxygen bottles in the home. "When these gases meet a flame," he said, "they erupt violently."

Arson investigator Mark Smith told jurors that no grill or cooker frame was found in the ashes, contradicting Linda's claim she'd stored a gas grill there.

Police Chief Aubrey Broadway testified that someone tipped him off about possible insurance policies with Linda as beneficiary. He said Linda gave him three different stories about the origin of the propane tank.

On cross-examination, Massey pointed suspicion toward Lula's daughter, Stacey, suggesting she may have been responsible. Broadway admitted that Lula didn't want her kids to know about the policies and confirmed reports that Stacey had stolen from Lula.

Still, doubts about Linda's guilt vanished when Brenda Driver testified. The fiery redhead described how Linda pretended to be Lula to obtain life insurance. Driver said Linda had claimed to be Lula's sister and said both were nurses. Driver met Lula, who was personable and spoke glowingly of Linda. After Lula died, Brenda called the number on the application and spoke with Linda, who pretended to be Lula's grieving sister. Brenda grew suspicious and later spotted Linda at Walmart, alive. She alerted authorities.

The final key witness was Charles Wayne Dunn. In a soft voice, head down, Dunn told jurors how Linda wanted him to kill Lula.

"Linda said she had given her medicine and seen her to bed," he testified. "She wanted me to make sure Lula was dead before I set the house on fire."

He described entering the home, speaking with Lula, helping her to bed, and giving her a pill. Then he waited until she was asleep, found the propane tank, and started the fire. Despite his criminal record and drug use, Dunn's testimony was chilling and believable. Massey tried to discredit him as a crack addict and liar, but the damage was done.

After Dunn's testimony, the court recessed. Linda headed to the ladies' room—the same restroom used by spectators. I followed a few moments later and found her by the sink.

"I believe that one over there is unoccupied," she said with a smile.

"Thanks," I said. "I've been meaning to talk to you. I'm from Los Angeles, and a friend of yours says hello."

Her face brightened. "Now, who would that be?"

"Eric Witmeyer," I replied. "He says you used to drive him around Memphis in your convertible."

She laughed. "Damn, I'd forgotten all about that. Eric was always something. Smart, a little wild. He's a lawyer now, isn't he?"

I nodded.

"You tell him that when this is all over, I'm coming out to LA. I want to go to Taco Bell with him."

She dried her hands and turned to go. "Tell him to get my bed ready in Los Angeles."

"How are you holding up?"

"Tired. It's hard to sleep in prison. I'm just glad my girls aren't there with me. Gary says Melanie is doing well in rehab. That's how this all started. Wayne Dunn got Melanie back on drugs, and I tried to get her away from him."

The deputy motioned that it was time to leave.

"Maybe we can talk more later," I said.

"Sure," she said.

Even after everything I'd seen, part of me still felt sorry for her. But I knew Linda Leedom was never coming to Los Angeles.

Conviction and Sentence

On August 31, 1999, five years after Lula Young died in a house fire, Linda Leedom was convicted of hiring Wayne Dunn to kill her best friend for $1 million in insurance proceeds. After her conviction, Linda was sent to a women's prison in Jacksonville. I'd only had one brief exchange with her during the trial, so I decided to track her down in Pearl, Mississippi, and interview her in prison.

It took me three hours to reach the Central Mississippi Correctional Facility. I hadn't called ahead—just showed up, hoping I could talk my way in. At the entrance gate, I was promptly denied. Years later, I realized how naïve that was. Prisons require formal procedures for visitation, but this was one of my earliest stories, and I figured I could talk my way inside.

I asked to speak with the warden. She was pleasant but firm—no entry without following the process, which would take several days. I explained I'd left my infant son in Los Angeles to come to Mississippi and needed to see Linda before flying back. The warden was sympathetic but unmoved. I kept pleading, telling her I wasn't there for an exposé—something that usually put prison officials on guard. She believed me, but still refused.

Frustrated, I blurted, "Do I have to call the governor to get permission to interview Linda Leedom?"

"You could try," she said, enjoying my irritation.

I rolled up the windows against the one-hundred-degree Mississippi heat, drove a short distance, and parked on the side of the road. My phone battery was dying, but I called the governor's office. I explained I was an attorney admitted to the California bar and now a journalist working on a book. They were kind and directed me to the Mississippi attorney general's office.

When I called, I was transferred to Attorney General Mike Moore's assistant, who had already heard from the governor's office. A few minutes later, I was told that the attorney general had granted me access and had personally called the warden.

I was stunned. In California, it was never that easy.

When I pulled back up to the prison, the warden stood, waiting with a smile.

"Well, I guess you went and called the governor. Bless your heart."

She directed me to park by a one-story building.

"We've already got a room ready for you to meet Miss Leedom."

I thanked her and was escorted inside. I was allowed a pen and paper, but no recording devices. The warden brought Linda in, then closed the door behind her. I expected a guard to remain nearby, but I was left alone with Linda.

She smiled, clearly glad to have company.

"Why would I have anything to do with Wayne Dunn, a guy who got my daughter Melanie hooked on drugs? And just so you know, Lula's daughter, Stacey, and her mom knew all about those insurance policies. The night before Lula passed away, Stacey was physically abusive to her, and I went over to stomp on her tail. Right after I was arrested, Stacey sued me civilly to try and get money. Buckethead, that kid is slow; left town because he's scared of his sister, and he should be."

She paused to catch her breath.

"Right before Lula's funeral, I felt betrayed. I had a feeling something wasn't right and suspected Stacey was involved. Mike Hancock, who was a good friend of mine, kept telling me I was imagining things. He's known me for years. If he didn't know I'd never do that, then nobody would. But Miss Flora suspected Stacey too. She didn't want that girl around. Right before the funeral, Stacey's husband, Steve, asked to see Lula's will. When Stacey saw she wasn't the beneficiary, words were exchanged at the funeral home."

Linda insisted she had given Lula's children several thousand dollars from her office, always in cash, but claimed those records had been taken. Over the years, she said, life had gotten bad for her and her family. Everyone in town believed she'd killed her best friend. She described an assault while awaiting trial.

"When I was in DeSoto County jail, someone kicked me in the ribs."

"That's awful. What happened?" I asked.

"Let's just say I'm not one to conform. I have a lot of medical problems. I passed out in the dayroom. My ribs were bruised, and they had to take me to DeSoto Baptist. I just kept throwing up blood."

"A lot of people are convinced, including the jury, that you killed Lula."

Linda's eyes welled with tears. "I still love her dearly. How can they think I hurt my friend? There was no real evidence. It didn't happen. It felt like a kangaroo driving the train that railroaded me through the justice system."

Our conversation ended with Linda promising to write. She said her attorney was already working on her appeal.

On September 29, 1999, Linda Leedom was sentenced to life in prison without the possibility of parole, plus a twenty-year consecutive sentence. She is still serving that sentence today.

Following her incarceration, I wrote to Linda in jail. Despite her lying, I still found myself liking her. She was smart, funny, and quick, and she reminded me a bit of my friend Eric. I was never able to reconcile my underlying fondness for Linda with the horrible crime that she committed against Lula, so the correspondence fell off over the years. I spent too much time with Lula's sweet family to forget what she'd done. When I thought about Lula struggling with her health, unable to move when the fire started, my fondness for Linda turned into disgust. I felt sorry that her life, filled with family and friends, had ended in this way—with her isolated from her husband and children and the grandchildren to come. It was sad, but it ceased to occupy my thoughts over the years. I never forgot about Lula, though, and her bad taste in friends.

CHAPTER SEVEN

The Final Performance: Robert Blake and Bonny Lee Bakley

Only six years after O.J. Simpson was acquitted of murdering his ex-wife, Nicole Brown Simpson, and her friend, Ron Goldman, in the first murder trial of the century, Los Angeles was treated to yet another high-profile murder case involving Robert Blake. It seemed eerily familiar. Yet another Hollywood star, just six years after O.J., standing handcuffed in a posh LA neighborhood; a white car speeding down a freeway with an armada of helicopters overhead; the LAPD announcement that a celebrity had been arrested for the murder of his wife. However, Robert Blake was no O.J. Simpson. And though Marcia Clark and other notable figures from the O.J. Simpson case popped up on TV to revitalize their fifteen minutes of fame, the arrest of the sixty-eight-year-old *Baretta* star would not play out like the original "trial of the century."

Blake, who began his career as a child actor, became best known for his role in the film *In Cold Blood* as well as for his Emmy-winning role in the television series *Baretta*. Although the popular series ended in May 1979, Blake was still quite famous when he married Bonny Lee Bakley in 2000. The two had been married just six months when Blake phoned the authorities on the evening of May 4, 2001, to report that he'd found his wife, Bonny Lee, dead in his car after having dinner at Vitello's Restaurant in Studio City, California.

On the evening of May 4, 2001, Blake and his wife, Bonny Lee Bakley, drove to dinner at one of Blake's favorite restaurants in Studio City, California, and the actor parked about one and a half blocks away from the restaurant. One source at the restaurant claimed that Blake normally used the valet, but that evening opted that evening to park almost two blocks from the restaurant behind a construction dumpster and under a broken street lamp. A waiter who served Blake hundreds of times, Christopher O'Brien that he would see Blake's car parked on the street in the same area as the crime scene..[14]

Blake told authorities that the couple dined at the restaurant, and after finishing their meal, they walked out together, and Bakley got in their car, but Blake realized that he'd left the gun

[14] Los Angeles Police Department Press Release, Thursday April 18, 2002, Robert Blake Arrested for the Murder of Bonny Lee Bakley. "On May 4, 2001, Bakley was found in the 11400 block of Woodbridge Street in North Hollywood, slumped in the front seat of her husband's car." That location is about a block and a half from the restaurant Vitellos, located in North Hollywood. A waiter at the restaurant, Christopher O'Brian, testified at the trial that Blake regularly parked in the spot about a block and a half from Vitello's restaurant and often called to make a reservation, contrary to the police's claims. https://www.cnn.com/2005/LAW/02/18/blake/

he used for protection in the booth where they'd had dinner. He ran back to the restaurant, retrieved his gun, and returned to the car.[15] Blake recalled to police that he was already in the driver's seat when he saw Bonny slumped in the passenger seat, bleeding from a gunshot wound. He then ran to a nearby house, banged on the door, and asked Sean Stanek, the owner, to call 911. He then returned to the car and vomited at the crime scene. One witness would later testify and confirm that they saw Blake sitting on a curb and "at one point he threw up" during the commotion following the shooting. However, there was another witness who testified at trial that Blake frequently threw up after meals. There were also allegations that Blake, a celebrated actor, actually made himself throw up to appear shocked by Bakley's murder.

When the police arrived at the Bakley murder scene, they cordoned off the area and pushed back the media and onlookers. The murder weapon, which was recovered in a dumpster, was an unusual vintage revolver and was subsequently determined not to be Robert Blake's gun. Blake was taken into custody by the police at the scene, and his hands were tested for gunshot residue, sampled, and released. The police did not take any measures to protect Blake's hands or clothing from gunshot residue contamination while he was in the police car and at the station.

Blake was carrying a .38-caliber pistol at the time of the murder. It was later determined that his gun was not the murder

---

[15] Waiter Christopher O'Brien, who was not working on the night of Bakley's murder, was called by the defense and testified at trial that Blake often parked in the spot he did that night and that he had called to make reservations at the restaurant on more than one occasion, contrary to the prosecution's claims that the actor always used the valet and that he never called to make a reservation. https://www.cnn.com/2005/LAW/02/18/blake/

weapon, but it was a source of the gunshot residue contamination on his hands and clothing. Police didn't take Blake's clothing into evidence until the next day, when it was collected by the police from Blake at his home. The clothing was placed by the police in an open cardboard box in the trunk of the police car for forty-eight hours before it was processed for gunshot residue.

Despite the distance, cameras captured a seemingly distraught Blake, pacing near the crime scene, head in hands, as he was interrogated by police. As the police collected evidence from the crime scene, the media presence grew, bringing back memories of the media circus that descended on O.J. Simpson following the murder of his ex-wife, Nicole Brown Simpson, and her friend, Ronald Goldman.

Blake immediately hired renowned Hollywood criminal defense attorney Harland Braun, whose clients included big names like Roman Polanski, Roseanne Barr, Gary Busey, and Chris Farley. Braun, who understood how to deal with the national media, immediately noted that the police considered Robert Blake to be a witness in the murder case, not a suspect or a person of interest. Meanwhile, Robert Blake's alibi—that he'd returned to the restaurant to get his gun—was ridiculed both by the media and the public.

The murder victim, Bonny Lee Bakley, was a forty-four-year-old mother of three who had only known Robert Blake for two years. The two met in 1999 at a jazz club in Studio City. It turned out that Bakley made her living by running a lonely-hearts scheme, sending nude pictures to men in exchange for money. Even after marrying Blake, she continued her business of sending nude photos to older, wealthy men, in the hopes that they would leave her their money when they died. She also had a criminal past. In 1989, she was convicted of drug possession in Memphis, Tennessee. FBI records showed that in 1994, while under investigation for fraud, Bakley told agents at the time that she'd used her then-thirteen-year-old daughter to seduce a man. And a year later, in 1995, she was convicted in Little Rock, Arkansas, for possessing false identifications, including possessing at least seven driver's licenses and five social security cards.

The LAPD quietly investigated the case while the public waited for Robert Blake to be arrested. The public was already convinced that Blake had killed his wife and that the LAPD would somehow botch the case, as they had with O.J. Simpson. But the police, mindful of the mistakes made by investigators in the O.J. Simpson case, were desperate to avoid accusations of a rush to judgment or claims that they'd mishandled the crime scene. On April 18, 2002, eleven months after the murder of Bonny Lee Bakley, the LAPD arrested Robert Blake at his home. The arrest was planned out to avoid anything reminiscent of O.J. Simpson's Bronco chase down the 405 freeway. With helicopters circling in the sky above Blake's home, officers surrounded the house and promptly took Blake into custody before driving him downtown for processing.

After Blake's arrest, the LAPD issued a press release stating that the charges against Blake would be presented at the actor's arraignment in court. The press release seemed to be written to dispel any notion that the police had rushed to judgment in charging Robert Blake with murder. During the nearly year-long investigation, detectives carefully examined more than nine hundred items of evidence linked to both Blake and Bakley, including letters, records, photographs, and other physical evidence. Detectives also interviewed more than 150 people. The investigation took detectives all over the United States, including several trips to the Northeast and the Southeast. In all, detectives spent time in some twenty states. No other case in the department's history has required such extensive travel.

The statement went on to note that "During the year-long investigation, detectives carefully examined over 900 items of evidence linked to both Blake and Bakley, including letters, records, photographs, and other physical evidence. Detectives also interviewed more than 150 people...detectives followed up on more than 150 clues, provided by citizens. All other possible suspects have been investigated and have been eliminated." It was a bold statement by the police to forestall the defense from later arguing that the investigation failed to question alternative suspects, particularly in light of Bonny's rather checkered past.[16]

Los Angeles police chief Bernard Parks made a statement that evening, noting, "The LAPD case has developed both physical and significant circumstantial evidence that Robert Blake killed Bonny Bakley." Parks stated that he would recommend that prosecutors charge the actor with one count of murder with special circumstances and two counts of solicitation of murder. The special circumstances, which police said were for "lying in wait," meant that Blake could face the death penalty.

A few days later, on April 22, 2001, Blake appeared in court and pleaded not guilty to one count of murder with the special circumstance of lying in wait, two counts of solicitation of murder, and one count of conspiracy. He was initially held in the LA County jail without bail. The actor was accused of two counts of

---

[16] Los Angeles Police Department Press Release, Thursday April 18, 2002, "Robert Blake Arrested for the Murder of Bonny Lee Bakley," Media Relations Section, Office of the Chief of Police.

solicitation of murder, conspiracy, and murder with the special circumstance of "lying in wait." The charges mandated that if convicted, Blake would face a death sentence.

The criminal complaint alleged that after dining at Vitello's in Studio City, Blake got Bakley into the passenger seat of his 1991 Dodge Stealth, opened the windows, came around to her side, and shot her twice in the head with a WWII-era Walther P38 nine-millimeter handgun before tossing it into a nearby dumpster. The complaint also alleged that Blake had plotted with his handyman and bodyguard, Earle Caldwell, forty-six, who allegedly drafted a list of items for the task that included "2 shovels, small sledge, crowbar, 25 auto, 'get blank gun ready,' old rugs, duct tape, Draino [sic], pool acid, lye, plant."

In their complaint against Blake's friend, Earle Caldwell, a former stuntman and handyman, supplied the actor with a small-caliber handgun and wrote up a list of supplies to use when disposing of Bakley's body. Prosecutors claimed that on one occasion, Caldwell hid in the bushes on the banks of a river in Parker, Arizona, armed with a handgun, and jumped out while Robert Blake and Bonny Lee Bakley were together. This incident allegedly occurred during a trip in March 2001 and was described in the complaint against Blake and Caldwell in the murder of Bonny Lee Bakley. Caldwell denied all the allegations and pleaded not guilty.

The list of supplies added more fuel to the public's conviction that Blake had killed his wife, prompting Blake's attorney, Harland Braun, to make a statement following his client's arraignment.

"That's a list that the police have had for almost eleven months," he said. "They have questioned Mr. Caldwell about that list, and while, actually, it looks suspicious, it is a bunch of supplies that were used to do pool cleaning and so forth. Mr. Caldwell already told police, and he has been questioned about that list repeatedly."

The prosecution made a motion to deny Blake bail, which included evidence of extensive phone calls allegedly showing that Blake had made dozens of calls to two stuntmen and a private investigator before Bakley's murder. Blake made the calls up until the afternoon of the murder to two stuntmen who claimed that Blake allegedly solicited them to kill Bakley. Prosecutors claimed that there was also a witness who would testify that Blake said he wanted Bakley to get an abortion, and if she refused, he could "whack" her. According to court documents, the witness also claimed that Blake called Bakley "the scum of the earth" and was under the false belief that she could use her pregnancy to get the actor to marry her. The prosecution also claimed the witness would testify that Roy Harrison, a stuntman, arranged meetings for Blake and two other men at Du-par's Restaurant and that Blake discussed ways his wife could be killed.

The prosecution's motion was successful, and Blake was held without bail. The actor's bodyguard, Earle Caldwell, was also charged and pleaded not guilty to conspiracy to commit murder. He was held on a $1 million bail.

At a press conference following the arraignment, Blake's defense attorney told reporters that Blake was innocent and claimed that Bakley's killer was still at large. Blake's children were standing behind him and had already visited. He added that although Blake wasn't happy about having to stay in custody during the entire proceedings, his client was relieved that his daughter with Bonny Lee, Rosie, would reside with his elder daughter from a previous marriage rather than being transported to New Jersey to live with Bonny's sister, Margerry.

As for claims from the prosecution that Bonny Lee told her sister Margerry that Blake was going to kill her, Harland replied, "It's probably what she claims Bonny told her, so if you think about it, how could Margerry testify about these events, because she wasn't there? The only way she could testify is by what she claims that Bonny told her."

The reporter countered, "So you would say her testimony is hearsay and inadmissible?"

"I wouldn't say it. The law says it."

"Would you say that she's lying?"

"That's what my client tells me. Or maybe the sister never said this."

Harland went on to summarize the case against Blake.

"This is over a child, and it's over money. You have to not lose sight of that fact. What happened was a father who was so devoted to a child that he was willing to sacrifice himself and marry someone he didn't want to marry. All of us agree on that. Now, most men who impregnated someone in the back of a jazz club would just pay some money and forget about the child. Both the prosecution and the defense agree that this is a father's love for his child. The only issue between us is did he…[kill] her to protect his child from what he thought was evil? We say that he didn't. He says that he didn't. The evidence will show that he didn't."

"The complaint says that Caldwell jumped out," the reporter stated.

"There are three people who were there. Blake has been questioned by police and he said that never happened. Bonny is dead and Caldwell says it never happened. So where in the world did they get that information? It didn't happen," Harland replied.

The spokeswoman for the prosecution, Sandi Gibbons, also issued a statement: "We're very anxious to get our evidence before the court and have a court decide what the evidence is. We're not going to talk about it outside of court. Mr. Blake has been arraigned and now so has Mr. Caldwell.... Hopefully, we'll get a preliminary hearing set very soon. As I said, we're very, very anxious to take this case to court and have the evidence tested by the judicial process.

"The evidence is what the evidence is. We're not going to talk about it outside of court. We think evidence needs to be tested in a court of law, not on a sidewalk."

Cary Goldstein, the Bakley family lawyer who'd also represented Bonny Lee in her initial paternity and postnuptial case against Robert Blake, told reporters that the prosecution had put together sufficient material to support their allegations against Blake.

"I don't think the DA's office is going to take any chances whatsoever in risking a loss in this case. The police department has to vindicate itself from prior investigations," he noted, referring not so obliquely to the O.J. Simpson case. "I might add that I am pleased with the judge's ruling about media in the courtroom. America needs to see that the wealthy and the celebrities in this country don't get away with murder."

One reporter pressed Goldstein about whether Margerry, Bonny's sister, had any knowledge about the murder.

"Because Margerry had such extensive contact with Bonny before her death, hours and hours on the telephone with Bonny telling Margerry extensive details, there was concern about

Margerry also being a victim," Goldstein replied. "You have to realize that Bonny told everyone that Blake was going to kill her."

A month after Blake's arrest, Harland Braun argued in front of Judge Nash for Blake's release on bail, presenting an alternate theory as to why gun residue was found on Blake's hands and clothing. Braun argued that the lab reports state that the source of the residue on Blake's hands and clothing was not known and that it could have come from the actor's other guns and not the gun found at the scene. Robert Blake, seated behind his lawyer, pleaded for his release, saying, "This is my right to fight for my life." He argued to the judge that he wanted to be able to help his lawyers prepare his defense, and that he was so severely dyslexic that he couldn't read any of the legal documents and needed to have them read to him. Although the judge ruled against releasing Blake on bail, he stated that he might release Blake on bail following evidence presented at the preliminary hearing.

CHAPTER EIGHT

Dinner and a Murder

Long before Robert Blake was arrested, I wondered if Blake had killed Bonny Lee. Given that my sources were already telling me that the murder weapon didn't belong to Blake, it seemed unlikely. As with any story I cover, I am committed to keeping an open mind until I have thoroughly reviewed all the facts. It's tempting to side with the source that's more persuasive, but often, sources have ulterior motives when providing information to a journalist. My legal background is helpful in those situations, because I was taught to be skeptical of all facts and arguments and to always examine a source's ulterior motives.

I was working at *Entertainment Weekly* in 2001 when Blakley was murdered. I began reporting on the story only days after the murder. My investigation in this case started with a visit to the restaurant where Bonny Lee and Blake had dined before her murder. There had been a lot of discussion in the media about why Blake had parked a block away from Vitello's rather than in the restaurant's sizable parking lot. When I arrived, I stopped at the exact place where Blake had parked that evening, thinking that the spot was sufficiently secluded for Blake to have killed Bonny Lee without being seen. However, it was possible, as Blake's lawyer suggested, that Blake was careful with his money and never paid for valet parking. He was a child of the Depression and had managed to build a decent fortune by making good investments and avoiding reckless spending.

Vitello's was entirely unremarkable, both in its décor and its food. It seemed apparent from our dinner that folks in the restaurant came more out of habit and nostalgia rather than for the cuisine. The restaurant was decorated in a traditional American Italian style, with small candles on the table, red and white table settings, and two levels of tables. The banquet—where Robert and Bonny dined on the night of Bonny's murder—was spacious and more perfunctory than romantic. Like the fare served at the restaurant, the overall décor was unexceptional. The patrons, on the other hand, were intriguing. Because of the restaurant's proximity to a number of studios, many of the guests worked nearby on television and movie sets. Vitello's was known to be a favorite of not only Robert Blake's but also other celebrities from that era, like Frank Sinatra, Sally Kellerman, Ana Ortiz, Tony Danza, Jason Alexander, and Michael Landon. According to one of the servers, the lunch crowd usually drew more customers. Evenings at the restaurant tended to be more relaxed, with mostly locals dining. But on the Saturday night I dined there, the restaurant was filled, given the publicity surrounding Bonny Lee's murder. Vitello's had become yet another infamous stop on the celebrity bus tour.

After dining at Vitello's, I investigated Bonny Lee and how she'd ended up married to Robert Blake. Bonny Lee's past was riddled with sex, crime, and celebrities. When I interviewed Margerry Bakley, Bonny's sister, for a pre-interview with ABC News, she told me that Bonny was both in a wildly dysfunctional family in New Jersey, her teenage years began with Bonny doing "stuff" with boys by the age of ten. Bonny spent most of her twenties and thirties targeting and exploiting older men in a wide variety of schemes. Right before hooking up with Blake, she'd stalked other famous people.[17]

At the press conference, Harland Braun, the attorney for Robert Blake, noted that Marjorie Bakley "...could very well believe that Blake killed her sister and want to fill in the evidence that would help the prosecution by making up things her sister said, I don't want to get into her background. She's been very nice to Robert Blake in her trip here, by basically putting his mind at ease that she's not going to try and take Rosie (Bonny's daughter) away."

I tried for several weeks to set up a meeting with Harland Braun, the renowned defense attorney representing Blake. We'd met socially over the years, and he knew he'd be receptive to me writing about the case. Harland agreed to meet with me at his office, agreeing to provide me with documents related to the case that would show there were other people, besides Blake, who wanted Bakley dead. Even though Blake hadn't been arrested, Braun knew that the media and the public had already convicted his client. He also understood the importance of media coverage

---

17 Margery Bakley is the author of *Blood Cold*, a book about her sister, Bonny Lee Bakley. During a pre-interview with me prior to her appearance on ABC *20/20*'s Robert Blake story, I also discussed Bakley's past with Bobby Memphis, who was married to Jerry Lee Lewis's sister when he first met Bakley.

in the Blake case and that it would help prove his client's innocence if the public knew more about the victim.

When I arrived at Harland's office, he opened a black binder.

"I've only released three pictures of her publicly. One is the one with the blonde hair, and two photos of her on the beach. But here are more than a hundred photos of her, mostly nude."

I glanced at the photos, most of which were very explicit nudes, including up-close pictures of Bakley with her legs spread. The photos were provocative, titillating, and graphic. She was nude, hanging on fences and over beds, breasts exposed and legs spread.

"These are pictures that she was currently sending out to guys, depending on who they were. It's disgusting stuff."

Harland explained that Bonny Lee Bakley was a predator—someone who sent nude photos of herself in various states of arousal to take money from men she'd met through personal ads. She was also someone who was obsessed with dating a celebrity. She'd compiled an address book with the names and contact information for at least seventeen celebrities, including Robert Redford, Sylvester Stallone, Chuck McCann, and others. She also kept what Harland called "a day log," notes that she kept on the men she was pursuing.

Braun handed me copies of a few pages of the log.

"This is her work for one day," he said, pointing to a list of typed names. "I mean, she's targeting all these men. She started as an Elvis Presley stalker when she moved to Memphis. This is her list."

As I read a few pages of the day log, I noticed that Bonny had typed out little notes about all the men she was pursuing, documenting her progress with each man. Some of the men were rich, some were famous. After one name, she'd typed "young and rich." Gary Busey, the actor, is followed by "Called as Bonny, left a message." The next notation stated, "Send # to Gary Busey, Tulsa, OK, mother is Virginia, will forward mail."

Under one section labeled "old and rich," she reminded herself to write to a man in Oklahoma, who "owns a 320-acre cattle ranch, if he finds a girl that is true, faithful & committed to him at his death, she would be financially secure." In a side note to herself, she reminded herself that she'd used the name "Sylvia" in her initial contact with the elderly man. In another entry, she reminded herself to send her number to Sugar Ray Lenard (at a post office in Alabama) and noted that she'd left a message for a man in San Francisco who "makes $170,000 a year, owns race horses and plays the stock market." She also made overtures to Robert DeNiro, Prince, dethroned Pentecostal preacher Jimmy Swaggart, *Hustler* publisher Larry Flynt, *Dukes of Hazzard* star James Best, Pat McCormick, Chuck Berry, and Frankie Valli, who Bakley claimed to have dated as a teenager.

Braun argued that Blake wasn't the killer, despite being tried and convicted already by the media, but the murderer was likely someone from Bakley's questionable past. Although Bakley had targeted all sorts of men over the years, her main targets seemed to be celebrities. I'd grown up in Los Angeles and knew that Hollywood was filled with people like Bakley, who were obsessed with pursuing famous people. As my editor, Benjamin Svetkey, and I wrote in an article for *Entertainment Weekly* about Bakley entitled "Dangerous Game," people like Bakley weren't simply groupies or stalkers.[18]

"What Bakley pursued with meticulousness and methodical precision wasn't so much cash as cachet, the reflected glory of being with a star. Any star would do—even one like Blake—whose star hasn't shown for the better part of a decade."

Svetkey would go on to write that while there was no specific diagnosis for this disorder in the current psychiatric lexicon, there should be, since "celebriphilia" is a familiar enough condition to those trained to look for it.

"You're talking about a woman who in one day targeted a whole bunch of different people," Harland explained. "She even targeted men overseas. This was her overall scam with all of them, and then she was sending out pornography to them. She sent out little nude pictures of herself. And, so she doesn't just target celebrities. This is a woman who targets all kinds of men."

According to Harland, Robert Blake met Bonny Lee and slept with her. He took her outside the jazz club and had sex with her in his truck at 3:00 a.m. in the parking lot. She would then come and stay at a motel near him, and he'd phone her and the two would have sex. It probably happened six or seven times.

"She was a stalker. I don't know how they got together, but sometimes when she called, he wouldn't bother to go over. He wasn't even really sure of her name."

Harland also noted that while Bonny was busy sleeping with Robert Blake, she was also attempting a relationship with Marlon Brando's son, Christian, who'd spent five years in prison

---

18 King, Gary C. "Who Murdered Bonny Lee Bakley?" Bonny the Celebriphiliac - Who Murdered Bonny Lee Bakley? - Crime Library, www.crimelibrary.org/notorious_murders/family/bakley/7.html. Accessed 13 Nov. 2025.

for shooting his half-sister's boyfriend. In an audiotape that Harland played for me, Bonny speaks about both men without any passion.

"You can hear on the audiotape how she wasn't sure she wanted him [Blake] or Christian or whatever," he noted. "She did a property profile on Blake before she met him. She got to know someone who knew him, and then they got introduced at a club. She uses sex. You've got all these women—they call them 'starfuckers.' I always wondered why these guys don't pay five hundred dollars for a vasectomy. This is nuts."

Blake and Bakley had sex on six to seven occasions.

"It wasn't just one night in the back of a truck," Harland said, trying to explain the relationship between the two. "Men are animalistic. They're not looking for emotional involvement, and Bonny used sex. He wasn't in love with her or anything like that. Here you have a woman who's got this entire world of sleaze. She's got no morals at all. And then she's going after what she wanted to be. You hear it on the audiotape. She wanted to be something. She even placed an ad on a billboard on Sunset Boulevard with her picture and her telephone number, but nothing happened. She's a disappointed celebrity."

Though Bakley managed to get pregnant by Blake, he wasn't her first choice. She'd spent ten years pursuing famed musician and singer Jerry Lee Lewis, who she alleged was the father of her daughter, Jeri. I called Jerry Lee Lewis after learning about how Bakley had pursued him, and he referred me to his long-time road manager, J.W. Whitten. After I got Whitten to agree to an interview, we met at a restaurant in Memphis, Tennessee, to discuss Bakley. Whitten met Bonny in Hartford, Connecticut, around 1980. After Jerry Lee Lewis performed a concert there, she was hanging around and went up to Whitten, asking him where he lived. She wanted to send him a card. When Whitten returned home to Memphis, there was a fifty-dollar mail order waiting for him from Bonny. She gave him the money, asking that he arrange a meeting with Jerry Lee.

Whitten never responded, but he recalled that Bonny would pop up at many of Jerry Lee's concerts, trying to get backstage and meet him. He recalled that she smiled a lot and was really friendly.

"She was all over us," he recalled. "She would always stay at the same hotels as us. She popped up at one of his birthday parties. Once she offered me money to tell her where he was. She thought she had a shot at being Jerry Lee's girlfriend," he said with a smile. "Do you know how many women wanted that job?"

When she failed to arrange a meeting, she moved to Memphis to be closer to Lewis. She repeatedly offered to pay Whitten if he would tell her where Jerry Lee was playing in Memphis. When he turned down her offer, she found another avenue to the famous singer, his sister, Linda Gail Lewis. She managed to become very good friends with Linda Gail, finally leveraging the friendship into a meeting with Jerry Lee Lewis. Despite her best efforts, the two never had a physical relationship.

"She came to this club, Hernando's Hideaway," Whitten remembered. "Jerry was there sometimes. She ended up saying that she was pregnant and Jerry was the father." Whitten laughed. "She was pretty persistent, but she was fighting a losing battle. They did a DNA test and it proved it wasn't Jerry's baby."

Whitten read in the paper that Bonny moved out to Los Angeles and pursued other celebrities like Dean Martin, Christian Brando, and Robert Blake.

"Sorry about everything that happened with Robert Blake. He fell into that trap. That could have been Jerry," Whitten said matter-of-factly.

Despite Bakley's criminal and notorious past, it didn't convince me that Blake was innocent. There was the matter of his alibi—that he'd left Bakley in his car and returned to the restaurant to get his gun. It was an alibi that had most people wondering why Blake hadn't managed to come up with a better story. I asked Braun how he was going to deal with Blake's somewhat unbelievable alibi.

"It's what happened," he shot back. "He just put his gun down to the side. Put the sweatshirt over it, put the sweatshirt on, and it fell to the ground. Gets back to the car, 'Oh my God, I left a loaded gun in there.'" Braun snapped his fingers. "Just like that, like most people would do who'd left a loaded gun in a restaurant."

It was an explanation, but I thought that there wasn't much Blake did that was like "most people."

I interviewed Harland Braun again in 2018 for a two-hour ABC *20/20* special about the murder. Even though he confessed to being tired of discussing the Blake case, he agreed to an interview. Braun was more candid this time regarding Blake, although he continued to insist on Blake's innocence. He began our discussion by focusing on the behind-the-scenes details about the LAPD's investigation of Blake. He recalled that when the LAPD first searched Blake's home, they refused to take any of the audiotapes or other evidence relating to Bakley's criminal efforts to steal from lonely older men. They said at the time that they didn't want any of the documents, blatantly dismissing Bakley's past scams and criminal behavior as irrelevant to her murder. It turned out that the LAPD later contacted Braun, demanding that he turn over all the evidence related to Bakley's criminal conduct. Braun found the request amusing, given their previous contempt for the documents, but he still volunteered to drive it to Parker Center. At that point, he said with a smile, the police rejected his offer, stating they couldn't guarantee his safety.

Braun, annoyed with the LAPD's behavior, orchestrated a creative way to get the documents to Parker Center. He contacted the *Los Angeles Times* and asked for a reporter from the paper to accompany him in his car while he drove the evidence to Parker Center. Braun again argued that the police were negligent in not taking the evidence in the first place. Bakley had defrauded so many men in her life; how could you know that Blake was the killer? He also pointed out that the police still were unable to answer the question of who killed Bakley, since it wasn't Blake.

"They were never able to prove that Blake had any connection to the murder weapon," he said, "nor were they able to prove that he'd hired someone to kill his wife."

The New Witnesses

After I'd spoken to Braun for the ABC News story, I discovered a friend of Robert Blake's that I hadn't interviewed when I initially covered the case. Brian Allan Fiebelkorn, who'd become friends with Blake after Bonny Lee's murder, had filed a lawsuit against the LAPD, alleging that the department and the lead investigator, Ron Ito, had ignored relevant evidence in the Blake case. He was committed to clearing Robert Blake's name. When I called to talk to him for the ABC News *20/20* show on Blake, he agreed to meet with me at his home in Laurel Canyon to talk about the case. I was, as usual, suspicious about Fiebelkorn's motives for speaking out on behalf of Blake, but the lawsuit intrigued me and I opted to meet with him.

Fiebelkorn and I met at his home in Laurel Canyon, only fifteen minutes from my residence in the Hollywood Hills. He had grown up in Hollywood and we immediately traded stories about various places in the area that we'd frequented as kids. I liked him immediately, but still remained skeptical about his friendship with Blake. This was Hollywood and when someone surfaces to do interviews in a high-profile case, one always has to wonder at the motive. Brian told me that he was ready to talk about his knowledge of Bonny Lee Bakley's death. He said that he'd tried to get the attention of the police before Blake's criminal trial, and they'd ignored him.

He explained that for years, the house across from his home in Laurel Canyon was occupied by a group of former stuntmen and other "Hollywood types" who made and sold methamphetamine. The police had tried and failed to close the house down over the years, and Brian had become close with some of the folks who lived there. He and his wife hosted an annual Christmas party every year, inviting all their neighbors over for dinner and drinks. He would exchange pleasantries with the men who lived there, and he got to know a few of them quite well.

After Bakley's murder, Brian read that police found the murder weapon in a nearby dumpster. When he read the description of the gun, a nine-millimeter Walther P-38 pistol, a German WWII–era weapon, he realized that he'd seen someone in his neighborhood with that type of gun in the weeks before Bakley's murder. Fiebelkorn told me that although the police interviewed many of his transient neighbors, they failed to interview him.

He first contacted District Attorney Steve Cooley. Convinced that he had evidence in the murder case, he contacted the police in 2004, claiming he had relevant information that Christian Brando was connected to Bakley's murder. He was interviewed at his place of business (Galpin Motors) by Detective Brian Tyndall, Lt. Donald Hartwell, and the lead detective on the case, Detective Ito.

Fiebelkorn would later file a complaint against the LAPD, and specifically against Detective Ito, alleging that the department convicted Robert Blake of the Bakley murder on the night she died, before any investigation had been conducted. He claimed that Detective Ito's investigation of Bakley's murder was based on a conclusion that he had already reached and intended to result in Mr. Blake's arrest and conviction. During his interview with me, Fiebelkorn explained that he was still angry that his testimony regarding the Bakley murder had been so easily dismissed by the police, arguing that Ito had attempted to suppress potentially exculpatory information and failed to investigate the credibility of prosecution witnesses and to pursue investigative leads that might have shown Blake to be innocent.

I was skeptical of Fiebelkorn's allegations and told him that I still didn't understand why he'd become so invested in proving Blake's innocence. He replied that when he came forward with evidence regarding the gun, the police treated him like he was a publicity-seeking liar and ignored the information he provided them during his lengthy interview. And, he added, they never turned over a report or summary of his interview to the defense, which would support his version of events.

"I told them that about three weeks before the murder, I'd seen a neighbor of mine, Mark Jones, carrying an old gun. I remembered chatting with Mark about the gun, saying that it looks old, dirty, and rusty. Mark had replied that he'd greased the weapon to avoid leaving fingerprints."

It wasn't until after the murder and facts about the case started to emerge that Fiebelkorn realized that most of the witnesses who were allegedly involved in the murder lived across the street from him.

"The major thing that you need to know about the murder is that there was a love triangle between Bonny Lee Bakley, Christian Brando, and Robert Blake, but Robert didn't know it, nor did I until after the murder," Brian explained to me while we sat in his home. "After Bonny and Robert's daughter was born in June 2000, Bakley told him that she wasn't sure that Rose was his daughter. Blake demanded she get a paternity test, but she refused, so he paid Bonny Lee one hundred thousand dollars to have the test. Once Blake found out that the baby was his, he called Marlon Brando and they had a very heated exchange," Brian claimed. "Blake told Brando, 'I know you wanted the baby to be Christian's to help him stay away from drugs, but the child is mine.' And Marlon got angry and threatened that if Blake didn't stay away from Bonny Lee and Christian, he wouldn't have a reason for living."

Fiebelkorn said that Brando's threats to Blake were not simply posturing. Blake knew that Brando had considerable influence with both the police and politicians. He was a wealthy man with influential connections. When his son, Christian, shot and killed Brando's daughter's fiancé, Brando used his connections to persuade the DA to cut a deal where Christian only served five years in prison. Given the threats by Brando, Blake hired Duffy Hamilton to be his bodyguard.

"The truth is that when Robert contacted Duffy Hambleton, he had no idea that Duffy was friends with Christian Brando or that he sold meth to him," Brian expounded. "While Robert was worried about Marlon Brando coming after him, he had no idea that Marlon, Christian, and several of his drug-addicted neighbors had discussed Bonny Lee's pregnancy on the phone and were incensed at her duplicity."

Fiebelkorn relayed that Christian Brando had a call with Hambleton, which the stuntman recorded, in which Brando said that somebody ought to put a bullet in Bonny's head. Another neighbor, Jerry Lee Petty, a Korean Air Force veteran, was also on the call. Fiebelkorn added that Petty had a large gun collection, including Walther guns.

Fiebelkorn was convinced that the call was evidence that Christian Brando, and not Blake, had paid to have Bonny murdered. Brian further asserted that Mark Jones, who committed suicide weeks after the murder, was likely paid by Christian Brando or Marlon Brando to kill Bonny Lee Bakley. Brian was certain the gun belonged to Jerry Lee Petty, and that Mark stole the gun from him, and after killing Bakley, couldn't live with himself.

"Jerry Lee Petty was a friend of Christian's, and when it turned out that Bonny had screwed over Christian, Jerry became extremely depressed and very withdrawn," Brian recalled. "He wasn't a druggie, but he was kind of like the Godfather of these guys. He let them stay at his home. He made his money off of renting these homes out to people who couldn't rent otherwise."

There was another witness, Diane Mattson, who claimed she'd been present during the call between Christian Brando and Hambleton, where Christian Brando stated he wanted to kill Bonny. During an interview on national television, Mattson's attorney, Brian Oxman, claimed that Mattson had overheard Christian Brando on a speakerphone say, "We need to put a bullet into Bonny Lee Bakley's head," and Duffy Hambleton said, "That's right." Diane had previously been in a platonic relationship with Christian Brando and had allegedly been present when the call happened. The judge in the criminal case ruled that while Christian Brando may have had a motive to kill Bakley, he lacked the opportunity to do so. Police confirmed that Brando was at home in Washington State on the night of Bakley's murder.

Woman with a Past

Though there were plenty of people willing to discuss Bonny's checkered past, there were very few who had anything nice to say. When I spoke with Margerry Bakley on the phone, she spoke lovingly about Bonny and their close relationship as well as about Bonny's children, who'd loved their mother. Their parents had a difficult relationship, and Margerry claimed they were verbally abusive and that her father molested Bonny. Shortly thereafter, their mother gave Bonny to their grandmother, Grammy Hall, to raise. Margerry believed that Grammy Hall, who was pathologically cheap, had loaned their mother some money, and the grandmother demanded Bonny as collateral on the loan. When Bonny lived with Grammy Hall, the woman wouldn't even let her wash regularly because she didn't want to pay for the water.

On one of the audiotapes made by Bonny, she spoke about events at Grammy Hall's house, saying, "I was the kid that everybody hated in school because I was poor and couldn't dress well. Everybody always made fun of me because I was a real loner type." Bonny continued, "So, you grow up saying, 'I'll fix them. I'll show them. I'll be a movie star.' And it was too hard because I was always falling for somebody. And I figured, why not fall for movie stars instead of becoming one?"

Margerry told me that Bonny's first marriage was to a Greek man who needed a green card. She was married at fifteen to Evageline Pulakis, a Greek national. "The asshole beat her, and so she had him deported." After turning twenty-one, Bonny married her first cousin, Paul Gawron, with whom she had two children, Holly and Glen. But after Bonny and Paul divorced, she became a single mother and needed an income. Margerry said that it was Bonny who taught her how to string someone along on the phone, alternately by cooing and giggling and then talking dirty.

Bonny also had another part of her business where she married older men who wrote her into their wills, and then she collected on their life insurance.

"She married this older guy named Thomas in Florida," Margerry said. "He was very smitten with her. She had herself made the beneficiary in his life insurance. And Bonny ended up getting a check for around eighty-two thousand dollars. She wrote me a postcard that said, 'That Thomas investment paid off.'"

Before she arrived in Los Angeles, Bonny had targeted Marlon Brando's son, Christian Brando, who was serving a jail sentence for the murder of his sister's fiancée.

"They began a correspondence," Margerry recalled. "The moment Christian got out of jail, she started pursuing him. They had a lot of things in common, like a messed-up family. She secretly began taking a fertility drug. She told both Blake and Christian that they were birth control pills."

After Bonny got pregnant, she wasn't sure if her baby was Christian's or Blake's. She'd call Margerry and ask who she should ultimately go with, Christian or Blake. "Bonny thought Blake was richer because he was old and he wouldn't be around for long," Margerry noted. "But she felt Christian was better looking and would inherit Marlon's money. But Christian did drugs and he also had a record."

I asked Margerry about a comment she'd made about Bonny, stating that she didn't agree with what Bonny was doing to Blake in terms of trying to get pregnant. Margerry admitted to me that there was a point where she felt sorry for Blake, but it changed when she learned about how Blake treated Bonny. Bonny repeatedly told her sister that Blake was always very uneven, nice one minute and screaming the next.

"There was something wrong with him, because you never knew whether he was going to be nice or nasty. He was always threatening to kill himself," Margerry said. "He'd say, 'I am going to kill myself. But don't worry. You're coming with me! I already got a bullet with your name on it.' He said it over and over again. And it wasn't something to be taken lightly. I warned Bonny that it was a threat."

A self-professed friend of Bonny's, Robert Stephanow, also claimed that Bonny's schemes were a direct result of her New Jersey childhood. Stephanow, who met Bonny when married to Jerry Lee Lewis's sister, Linda Gail said that Bonny confided in him that she learned how to make money off of older men at an early age.

"When she was a teenager, she said they had a pool for girls but allowed older men to come in and swim there. The men would hit on the girls," Stephanow recalled. "She learned she could get anything from men as long as she played up to them. She started a mail-order business and would post ads for men who were generous and looking to meet up. Her first cousin, Paul, would take the nude pictures of her that she would send out to the men. Once they were hooked, she'd charge them to get more photos. When she finally made it to Hollywood, she tried to get work. She even put up a billboard on Sunset with her number. But she wasn't a good actress, and she couldn't sing, so she went back to looking for a rich guy to marry and kept sending out those nudes for money."

Margerry learned about her sister's death when reporters showed up at her apartment door in Dover, New Jersey, shortly after midnight on May 5, 2001.

"CNN was on," she recalled tearfully. "My mother was on the other line, and the doorbell was ringing, and it's *Star* magazine. And my mother says, 'The son of a bitch shot her. He killed her. She's dead.' And as she was saying that, CNN was broadcasting the loading of her body into an ambulance."

Margerry remained convinced that Robert Blake killed her sister. She claimed that Bonny was going to take the baby away from Blake, and when he heard her talking about her plans on the phone, he lost it.

"He knew that he had to stop her before she took Rose," Margerry insisted.

After Blake was arrested without bail, some outlets reported that he was suicidal and wouldn't last in jail. I spoke with Harland Braun and asked after Blake. Harland said Blake was doing the best he could and then shifted to talk about how the publicity about the murder was affecting Blake's right to a fair trial.

"There have been cameras at every phase of this case, and high publicity along with immense public speculation. You have to remember that this case started with Mr. Blake's very public arrest, which generated a splash of publicity," Harland said. "Did you know that he offered to turn himself in to the police the day before?"

I said nothing.

"Right. You didn't know. No one reported that."

His monologue picked up intensity regarding Blake's actual arrest.

"Just remember that when Robert Blake was arrested, the police chief for the LAPD publicly stated, 'The Bakley murder has been solved.' He publicly and soundly branded Blake as guilty. So, this case started off with the police generating publicity. The police establishment started off generating condemnation of my client before he even went to court for his arraignment. It's already been devastating to Blake's right to a fair trial."

A reporter at the conference pointed out that Bakley's sister, Margerry, said Bakley knew that Blake was trying to kill her and would testify to it. Braun said that anything Margerry heard from her sister was hearsay, and she wouldn't be able to testify about it, or, he posited, maybe Bonny Lee Bakley never said that. Braun then gave a summary of what really happened between Blake and Bakley.

"This is over a child, and it's over money," Braun said. "You have to not lose sight of the prosecution's theory or take our theory of what happened. What happened was that a father was so devoted to his child that he was willing to sacrifice himself to marry someone he didn't want to marry. All of us will agree on that. It's over a child. Most men who impregnated someone in the back of a jazz club would pay some money and forget about the child. So, both the prosecution and the defense agree this is a father's love for his child. The only issue between us is did he go further than marrying her to sacrifice himself? Did he kill her to protect his child from what he thought was evil? He says he didn't, and I think the evidence will show that he didn't."

Blake was feeling the same thing and wanted desperately to speak publicly about the case and to proclaim his innocence. He was approached by several major networks to do a televised jailhouse interview. He ultimately agreed to do one with ABC News. When Harland Braun learned that the interview would take place, he resigned, citing to the court that he and his client disagreed on the handling of media relations. Following Braun's resignation, other attorneys who were commenting on the case took the opportunity to criticize Braun for his unwillingness to allow Blake to give interviews to the press. Braun responded forcefully to the criticism.

"If you don't answer all the questions, you look guilty," Braun replied to numerous media outlets. "If they cut you off before you answer, you look guilty. If you do well, they say you're just an actor. It's a no-brainer."

Following Braun's resignation, Blake hired Jennifer Keller and the acclaimed defense lawyer Thomas Mesereau, who'd successfully represented Mike Tyson during a rape investigation in 2001, where the charges were dropped. Mesereau told the media that he'd taken the Blake case for very specific reasons.

"I decided that Robert Blake needed my support and representation. I also decided he was a good person who had been vilified and mischaracterized in the media for two years, and I felt that I could and should work to change that."

Mesereau's first move was to stop a jailhouse deposition of Blake in the civil case filed by the Bakley family. Mesereau called the deposition a "clown show" and a "circus" filled with improper procedures. Los Angeles County Superior Court Judge David M. Schacter fined Mesereau for "engaging in unprofessional personal attack on opposing counsel" during a January 15 deposition in the civil wrongful death lawsuit filed by Bakley's four children. Although he paid the fine, Mesereau continued to aggressively defend Blake.

Blake's Preliminary Hearing

Normally, a preliminary hearing presents very limited opportunities for a defendant. The preliminary hearing under California criminal law provides that after a felony complaint is filed, the defendant is automatically entitled to such a hearing. The hearing is like a trial in a lot of ways, but there are some distinctions. In a criminal trial, the state must meet a burden of proof that the defendant is guilty beyond a reasonable doubt. However, in a preliminary hearing, the state just needs to meet a standard that there is probable cause for the defendant to proceed to trial based on the evidence presented. Most preliminary hearings turn out to be rather a formality, with the judge ultimately deciding there is enough evidence to send the case to trial. Therefore, I wasn't expecting much to happen at Blake's preliminary hearing. I figured that the fireworks wouldn't start until the trial. I was wrong.

Judge Nash opted to allow cameras in the courtroom for the preliminary hearing, giving the public a chance to see the state's evidence against Blake. The prosecution opened with evidence that demonstrated that Blake's motive for killing Bonny Lee was strong: she'd trapped him into marriage, was attempting to extort him over custody of their daughter, Rose, and he had desperately wanted out of the marriage. Prosecutors argued that Blake had first solicited others to commit the murder, but when they refused, he killed Bonny himself.

The state called several witnesses who claimed that Blake had solicited them to kill Bonny Lee. Gary McLarty, one of the stuntmen allegedly solicited by Robert Blake, testified that shortly after the murder, he went to LAPD's North Hollywood station and told police about the solicitation, because it was "eating inside of me." McLarty claimed Blake offered him ten thousand dollars to kill some unnamed woman and asked to meet in March 2001. Though the two men weren't friends, according to McLarty, he knew Blake from working with him on *Baretta*. Blake also allegedly asked McLarty if he had a silencer.

"Then he started to show me how one might come in at night and literally bump her off," McLarty said. "He said he wanted to pay ten thousand dollars."

McLarty testified at the preliminary hearing that Blake told him about possible plans for killing this woman. One way to kill her was for somebody to sneak into her room in the guesthouse at night and shoot her. He claimed that Blake told him how to get into the guesthouse without Bonny Lee knowing. The next plan Blake suggested was for Blake to take her out to dinner, and for someone to lie in wait and ambush her in a car after the two finished.

"Just about what [actually] happened," McClary testified. "He would eat dinner one night, go back to the car, and then leave, and that would give someone time to dispose of her that way."

Three days later, when Blake called back, McLarty claimed he told the actor that this woman hadn't done anything to him, so he wasn't going to murder her.

In a wave of blistering cross-examination, Blake's lawyer, Tom Mesereau, focused on the stuntman's lack of credibility. He asked about an incident in which McLarty had shot and killed a housemate. The lawyer pressed McLarty, asking what he'd told the police at the time of the shooting. Mesereau ultimately got McLarty to admit that he'd initially lied to police and gotten a friend to cover for him, essentially destroying the witness's credibility. The defense lawyer then switched to McLarty's history of drug abuse, questioning the stuntman about his violent drug addiction and his poor memory and documented mental problems. As Mesereau peppered the stuntman with questions about what he'd told police about the Blake meeting, McLarty struggled to remember significant details, with parts of his testimony contradicting his early statement to the police.

Next up for the prosecution was Ronald "Duffy" Hambleton, the stuntman who'd told police that Blake offered him money to kill his wife. He claimed that Blake ran several potential scenarios for how Hambleton could kill his wife, but in every scenario, Blake placed himself at the crime scene following the murder. Hambleton mentioned to the actor that his presence at the crime scene could be risky, but Blake told him not to worry, stating, "I am an actor." When Hambleton asked why Blake simply didn't buy Bakley off, the stuntman claimed the actor became angry and agitated. According to Hambleton, Blake said that there was no other way to get out of the situation except by killing Bakley.

During cross-examination, Blake's lawyer attacked the witness, suggesting he'd invented these incriminating stories about Blake to curry favor with the police. Mesereau noted that Hambleton stuck with the same story for six months when interviewed by police, stating that he knew nothing about any plan by Blake to have him kill Bonny Lee. Hambleton also admitted under cross-examination that he told the police during several initial interviews that he actually met with Blake to discuss a motorcycle movie project.

Mesereau also wanted to chat about how Hambleton had informed the police that the other stuntmen who claimed to be witnesses were a "bunch of flakes" who weren't credible enough to build a case against Blake.

Mesereau asked what made Hambleton change his story on November 29, 2001, and tell police that Blake wanted his wife "snuffed."

"I finally made up my mind, telling it like it is, probably the right thing to do.... I believe it is morally right."

Mesereau ended the cross by asking Hambleton why his account of Blake's murder pitch changed three times in police statements, effectively raising concerns about Hambleton's very detailed statements.

After Hambleton had been dismissed from the witness stand, the judge announced a brief recess. Thomas Mesereau stepped outside to address reporters. He told those present that he'd found so many holes in Hambleton's story that it was now "Swiss cheese," adding that it was "just another episode in a case that's been glamorized into something it's not. It's a case made out of Hollywood tabloids, not reality.... When you look at the evidence and put it under a microscope, there's nothing there."

The prosecution's LAPD gunpowder expert, Steve Dowell, testified that Robert Blake's hands had tested positive for lead, one of the main components of gunshot residue. But during cross-examination, Dowell admitted that any person with either a "hobby or occupation" involving guns could test positive for the presence of lead. Blake's defense established that the defendant had told the police at the crime scene that he had collected firearms and that he'd gone back to the restaurant to retrieve his loaded gun.

Lead on the hands "could be from that association and not necessarily the recent discharge of a firearm," Dowell stated when questioned about whether the residue was from a fired gun. The gunpowder tests were further undermined by the defense when another LAPD crime scene investigator testified that the kit used to test Blake is unreliable for suspects known to handle firearms.

The prosecution's expert also testified on direct that there were particles of gunshot residue on Blake's boots. He testified that he'd identified "one highly specific particle" of gunshot residue and "several other consistent particles." He also testified that the majority of the particles contained only lead, and did not present with the other components of gunshot residue and that those particles could have been produced by "environmental factors."

Debra Cowal, a criminalist, also offered testimony helpful to Blake's defense on cross-examination when she admitted that those particles found on Blake could have come from other sources such as clothing or the gun and holster that he was carrying that evening and that the particles could be completely unrelated to Bakley's murder.

There was also the issue of the weapon that was used to murder Bakley. After the coroner's criminalist, Steven Dowell, testified that particles of gunshot residue were found on Blake's clothing, he admitted on cross that those particles could have come from sources other than the murder weapon. It was an admission that because Blake was a gun collector who'd also handled his weapon that night, it was impossible to determine the source of the particles found on Blake's hands or clothing.

The defense also used the preliminary hearing to discredit the state's investigation of Bonny's murder—an argument that brought up memories of the botched investigation of the O.J. Simpson case. The defense claimed that the LAPD's investigation of the murder had been tainted by the presence of former *Los Angeles Times* reporter Miles Corwin, who'd been given access to not only the crime scene, but also Robert Blake's home.

LAPD detective Ronald Ito took the stand for the prosecution. He confirmed that police had provided Miles Corwin with information to write a book about Bonny Lee Bakley's murder from the time her body was found on May 5, 2001, until two weeks before the preliminary hearing began. Ito testified that he once introduced Corwin as his "partner," but when the potential witness asked for identification, Ito acknowledged that Corwin wasn't with the LAPD. Ito also admitted on the stand that Corwin had been at the crime scene and had been given access to evidence before defense attorneys. However, he strongly played down Corwin's participation, claiming that it had not hurt the integrity of the investigation.

When Mesereau began cross-examination, he quickly got Detective Ito to admit that he was the one who took the unusual step of allowing a writer to participate in the Blake investigation. When questioned about Corwin's history with the LAPD, Ito admitted that the LAPD had cooperated with Corwin on other criminal investigations. Detective Ito claimed that he had been ordered by LAPD Chief Bernard Parks to let Corwin tag along. When asked whether Corwin had potentially contaminated evidence at the crime scene, Detective Ito claimed that the crime scene was secured immediately when the police arrived. Prosecutors objected to the line of questioning, but Judge Nash refused to stop Mesereau, noting that Corwin's presence at the crime scene had the potential to contaminate evidence and was fraught with other problems.

Mesereau pressed about whether Corwin touched anything at the crime scene, with Detective Ito claiming that Corwin didn't touch anything without permission.

"He didn't touch blood. He didn't touch trace evidence; he didn't touch fibers; he didn't touch clothes. I know that he didn't touch those items."

"How do you know? You weren't there," Mesereau stated, referring to the fact that Ito arrived at the crime scene after Corwin.

The defense inquired as to whether Corwin was properly garbed at the crime scene, eliciting from Ito that Corwin had not worn plastic gloves at either the crime scene or Robert Blake's home. It was also established on cross-examination that there was no video of Corwin either at the crime scene or during the search of Robert Blake's home. Detective Ito chalked that up to a fluke, which raised questions about what Corwin was doing at both locations.

The video of the search of Blake's home included a close-up shot of a box of nine-millimeter bullets. Since Corwin wasn't on camera during the search of Robert Blake's home, the defense asked the detective if the author had been shown the box. Ito answered that he had. The box of nine-millimeter bullets was confiscated by police, but three bullets were missing, raising potential issues about whether Corwin had taken them.

Mesereau questioned Detective Ito about whether he knew that Corwin was writing a book about the murder that cast Corwin as the main character. Ito replied that he was aware.

"Will bringing Mr. Corwin around get you in a book or a movie?" Mesereau asked.

"A book for sure," Ito said, adding that he had no desire to be part of a book.

Ito managed to say that he never asked Corwin to be at the scene, but that fact only pointed to the fact that Corwin didn't feel that he needed to contact Ito before showing up at a closed-off crime scene, suggesting previous collaboration between the detective and the author.

After the very successful preliminary hearing in which the defense established several serious flaws in the prosecution's case, Mesereau ended the hearing by successfully convincing Judge Nash to reverse himself and set bail for Robert Blake. Blake emerged from prison as a ghostly version of his prior self, diminished in size and personality. A close friend of Robert Blake's would later tell me that when Robert Blake came out of prison, he was even more damaged than before he was arrested.

"One of the things that affected me about Robert, you see a very wounded animal," he told me during his interview. "He was already a very tender and wounded animal. You have to understand the impact of being put in solitary confinement has on a person; it changes you and makes you different. Being put in solitary confinement hurts deeply, and if it is connected to childhood trauma, like it was for Robert, it hurts even more. Although Robert was never my role model, he is a man who was put in a concrete box for a year, and that changes you, and it changed him. If you get put through this sort of legal tree chipper, you don't come out a Sequoia."

Following the preliminary hearing, Blake and Thomas Mesereau parted ways, the lawyer citing irreconcilable differences as the cause of the breakup. Blake hired another respected criminal lawyer, Gerald Schwartzbach, to start trial preparation.

CHAPTER NINE
The Circus

The criminal trial of Robert Blake differed from the O.J. Simpson trial in that, prior to opening statements, Judge Darlene E. Schempp barred television cameras from most of the high-profile trial, signing an order that allowed coverage only for the opening and closing statements and the verdict. In the days before the trial's start, the pundits took to the air to predict that, unlike O.J. Simpson, Robert Blake would be convicted of murder and spend the rest of his life in prison. But those pundits, much like the ones that covered the O.J. Simpson trial, missed that the prosecution had yet to present evidence that tied Robert Blake to the murder weapon found at the scene. Before the defense even began their case, prosecutors were unable to definitively place the murder weapon in Blake's hand or prove that the gunpowder residue found on his clothing was from firing that weapon.

The absence of cameras inside the court failed, however, to tamp down the media circus outside the courtroom. Even before the lawyers arrived at the courthouse in Van Nuys, I glanced out the window from the fifth floor of the courthouse and surveyed the area from above. The lawn and pathways in front of the courthouse were littered with various colored media tents, all stuffed tightly together, with most within merely a few feet of each other. Off to the left of one tent from KFI 640, there was a cappuccino and espresso stand surrounded by people chatting and drinking their coffee. On the far right were two umbrellas, one of which had "Shofar hotdogs" on the top and the other "Bagels."

I noticed a gray-haired man in a sharply tailored suit walking from one tent to another, handing out business cards. He was likely one of the many attorneys on the scene, trying to book a gig with the various outlets. There were also the reporters, stalking the area, stopping anyone who looked as if they might be associated with Blake's trial. When I walked past the tents on my way into the courthouse, someone had even stopped me, aggressively asking if I was someone involved with the Blake trial. I can still recall the look of disappointment on the reporter's face when I identified myself as a journalist covering the trial. Fortunately, his disappointment was short-lived, as he got a prosecution investigator to stop for an interview only moments later.

When the trial finally began, most of the reporters remained outside, able to watch the opening statement on small television sets under their respective tents. I sat in the back of the courtroom, watching intently as Deputy District Attorney Shellie Samuels stood up to begin her opening statement. She began by focusing on motive, making the case about why Robert Blake was the person with the strongest motive to kill Bonny Lee Bakley. She told the jury that Blake literally despised Bakley, regarding her as a lowly con artist from a very trashy family who'd trapped him into marriage by getting pregnant. When Bakley refused to take a paternity test or to have an abortion, the prosecutor said Blake became desperate to get full custody of their daughter, Rose, and remove Bakley from his life. She underscored her point by playing the jury an audio recording of Blake telling a friend visiting him in jail, "Rosie is safe. Those monsters will never get her, that other family."

Samuel outlined that Blake's desire to rid himself of Bakley drove him to offer at least three people a great deal of money to murder his wife. She claimed that the state would show that Blake called Gary McLarty, a stuntman that he'd worked with in the past, and offered him ten thousand dollars to kill Bakley. The two met on several occasions, but the stuntman refused. Blake offered a second man twenty-five thousand dollars to murder his wife, but the man turned him down. He also contacted Frank Minucci, a small-time crook who lived in NYC, that Blake wanted to kill Bakley and said that a blank check awaited him if he came to California to kill Blake's wife.

Finally, the prosecutor argued, after being repeatedly unable to hire someone to kill Bakley, the actor realized that the only solution was to do it himself. As for Blake's alibi that he was not there when Bakley was shot in the head, Samuels claimed that no one from the restaurant ever saw Blake return to the place to retrieve anything from his table, noting that while that may have been his plan, he was likely too upset by murdering Bakley to return.

The defense started strong, with Gerald Schwartzbach pointing out the holes in the prosecution's case against Blake. He noted that while the prosecution claimed that no one wanted Bakley dead more than Blake, the reality was that Bakley's past fraudulent activities had hurt so many people in the past that there was a laundry list of people who wanted her dead. Schwartzbach also drilled down on a key evidentiary element missing from the prosecution's case, specifically that the People had failed to tie the defendant to the murder weapon. They had no eyewitnesses, no blood evidence, or DNA, the lawyer told the jury. However, the lawyer posited, prosecutors still claim that Blake pulled the trigger. To make that case, Schwartzbach explained, they have a series of drug-addicted, mentally unstable stuntmen who will testify that Blake attempted to hire them to kill Bakley.

Unfortunately, the lack of cameras in the courtroom during witness testimony left the public with a dearth of information about any weaknesses in the People's case against Blake. When the first two stuntmen were called to testify, the media reported that their direct testimony against Blake was strong and filled with details. Sitting in the courtroom, my reality was quite different. I saw Gary McLarty, one of the stuntmen who'd testified at the preliminary, essentially destroyed on cross-examination by the defense. Schwartzbach got McLarty to admit that he'd lied under oath at the preliminary hearing about his drug history. At the hearing, McLarty claimed he'd experimented with drugs but rarely used them. At the trial, McLarty was forced to admit that even after Blake's arrest, he continued to use drugs, which led him to think that his house, car, and cell phone were bugged; that people were tunneling under his home, and that the lead detective in the Blake case, Ronald Ito, was after him. He further admitted that his delusions from excessive cocaine and marijuana use became so severe that he was admitted to a psychiatric facility.

Later in the proceedings, the defense continued to attack McLarty's credibility by calling both McLarty's estranged wife, Karen, and son, Cole, to testify. Both Karen and Cole testified that his cocaine abuse had resulted in McLarty having delusions that someone was bugging his phone, that people were watching him from a satellite, and that there was a tracking device on his motorcycle. Cole specifically testified that he was concerned that his father's delusions may have driven him to tell the police inaccurate information about Robert Blake.

Karen also told the jury that McLarty had told both her and Cole that Blake had offered ten thousand dollars not to murder Bakley, but rather to follow a man stalking Bakley and to hurt him. On cross-examination, the prosecution wondered why, if Karen was so worried about McLarty's excessive drug use, she didn't report his cocaine abuse to his co-workers.

Karen listened attentively and then answered matter-of-factly, "There are a lot of people who do cocaine in Hollywood, and it's not looked upon as being that horrible."

The next stuntman witness, Duffy Hambleton, was predictably solid on direct examination, with the stuntman telling the jury that he'd worked with Blake in the 1970s but had not seen the actor for more than two decades. He agreed to get together when the actor called, as he was always looking for work. When Hambleton arrived at the Studio City diner to meet with Blake in March 2001, he realized that the meeting wasn't only about work. Hambleton repeated his testimony from the preliminary hearing, adding a few more details, stating that Blake had suggested various scenarios for killing Bakley, including one outside Vitello's, the restaurant where Bakley was killed two months after Blake allegedly raised the subject with Hambleton. Blake proposed other locations to Hambleton for Bakley's murder, including Laughlin, Nevada, because the couple liked to camp in Jawbone Canyon.

The stuntman also claimed that Blake suggested yet another ambush scenario, where the stuntman could hide in Blake's van nearby the parking lot and take care of things when Blake and Bakley left the restaurant. He claimed that the actor also suggested that the stuntman could kill Bakley at the guesthouse where she lived.

When the stuntman refused Blake's offer, he testified that the actor said, "Well, if you're not going to do it, then I sure as hell am." (It turned out that on the day of his arrest, Blake was wearing a sweatshirt with the phrase "I survived Jawbone Canyon.")

Under cross-examination by Schwartzbach, Hambleton was a great deal less effective. When he was asked by the defense to explain why he didn't report to the police that Blake intended to kill his wife, Hambleton responded that after several meetings with Blake, he was frightened for his family, and he opted not to contact the police because he was frightened of Blake. He told the jury that he wanted "to get out of it any way I could."

Schwartzbach also chipped away at Hambleton's credibility, asking the stuntman about his recent arrest. Schwartzbach repeatedly attacked the witness's credibility, getting the stuntman to admit to being arrested after a psychotic episode triggered by his meth use. Hambleton had recently pleaded guilty to one misdemeanor count of brandishing a weapon and had been sentenced to ninety days in jail. During that incident in 1999, Hambleton had called 911, believing that his ranch was under siege by twenty gunmen. Hambleton claimed that after the incident at the ranch, he stopped using meth. Schwartzbach insinuated that not only had Hambleton lied about not using meth after the incident, but he'd also concocted the story about Blake soliciting him to curry favor with the authorities.

Prosecutors next turned their attention to the gunshot residue evidence compiled at the scene and after the search of Blake's home. Although gunshot residue was found on Hollywood actor Robert Blake's hands and clothes, the prosecution's forensic expert, criminalist Steven Dowell, testified that the defendant could have gotten the residue from guns that were not the murder weapon, including the actor's gun. Dowell stated that the sticky gun residue can easily be transferred from surface to surface, that it can cling to clothing for years, and that it was not a reliable indicator of whether the actor fired the gun that killed Bonny Lee Bakley. He also noted, however, that while the forensic evidence does not prove that Blake fired the murder weapon, it also does not exclude the defendant. The defense expert, Celia Hartnett, testified that Blake had significantly less GSR on his hands than would be expected if he had fired the weapon that killed Bakley.

The prosecution attacked the lack of blood spatter on Blake's clothing with Steve Englert, their blood spatter expert.[19] Englert testified that for blood to transfer to a shooter's clothing, the shooter would have to have shot the victim at a very close range. He also explained to the jury that the fact that no blood was found on Blake's clothing did not eliminate him as the shooter.

As for DNA linking Blake to the murder, another expert, Michael Mastrocovo, who collected evidence at the crime scene,

[19] "6.01 Blood Spatter." n.d. Accessdl.state.al.us. https://accessdl.state.al.us/AventaCourses/access_courses/forensic_sci_ua_v17/06_unit/06-01/06-01_learn_text.htm.

described a mucus-like substance on the car door, claiming the substance was not from Bakley, nor was it from Blake.

Ultimately, despite two years of investigation into Bakley's murder, the lack of evidence from the Bakley crime scene was shocking, especially given that it was processed on the actual night of the victim's murder. LAPD had failed to find any forensics, fingerprints, blood spatter, or eyewitnesses that supported the prosecution's theory that Blake had shot Bonny Lee Bakley in the head.

Unsurprisingly, in March 2005, Blake was found not guilty of first-degree murder since the prosecution failed to ever place a gun in his hand or to link the murder weapon to him. He was also found not guilty on the charge of soliciting someone else to murder Bakley. The stuntmen witnesses had serious issues with their credibility, which was wildly evident from the preliminary hearing, long before the trial. The jury deadlocked on the second solicitation charge, and the judge ultimately dismissed the charge. However, just a few months later, he went to trial in a civil wrongful death suit brought by Bakley's children, where the jury found him liable for her death. Blake was ordered to pay Bakley's children $30 million in wrongful death damages. The award was cut in half by the appellate court, and the parties then entered a confidential settlement.

Long after I finished working on the Bonny Lee Bakley story for ABC News, I got a phone call in the spring of 2019 from Robert Blake. Blake's voice was instantly recognizable as well as his choice of vocabulary. It was like I'd stepped into an episode of his show *Barretta*, albeit without the "don't do the crime if you can't do the time" refrain. Robert was very polite, less sure of himself than he'd been in the *20/20* interview. He told me that he was thinking of getting back in the business. He was eighty-five at the time, but still wanted to do some acting gigs, make some money. He needed me to help him get out the word.

I was somewhat stunned by the request. His friend Brian Fiebelkorn had told me a while back that Robert Blake liked the special on Bonny Lee Bakley, and that he was going to call. I incorrectly assumed that if he did call, it would simply be to thank me since I'd interviewed and booked a lot of the guests. However, Robert was under the mistaken impression that I was an agent and able to get him work. I politely explained that I was just a journalist and that I had no ability to procure auditions or work for him. He was sorry to have bothered me. He didn't realize that I was only a journalist. The only part made me smile, because I was sure that Robert Blake never had much use for journalists. He ended the call with a quick goodbye, and I sat there for a moment. I felt badly for Robert Blake. He'd worked since he was a small kid, earning money and ultimately respect and fame. The trials had taken their toll and long before he was eighty-five, there was little hope of him resurrecting his career. It had been mostly over even before he met Bonny Lee Bakley. I understood his call to me. He'd had a brief taste of attention and time in front of the cameras, and he wanted more. I secretly wished I could have given him another moment under the lights to savor, but after all, I was only a journalist and his story was over, awaiting only the footnote of his death, which would come in March 2023.

CHAPTER TEN

No Good Deed: The Murder of Amie Harwick

The murder of Amie Harwick is a bit more personal than some of the other crime stories that I've covered in the book. Amie Harwick's murder occurred in the Hollywood Hills, extraordinarily close to my home. The murder had happened on Valentine's night, when Amie, thirty-eight, had returned to her home after attending a burlesque show and having dinner with friends. Though I didn't know Amie personally, I was familiar with some of the folks who lived on Mound Street and had often strolled up that street to avoid the traffic of Upper Vine, where my home was located. When I heard about her murder, I walked up to Mound Street just to look at her house and try to see what had happened. Her Spanish-style home was typical for the Hollywood Hills, with white walls, blue accents, and an outdoor balcony, just off the master bedroom, which offered expansive views of the city's famous lights. I stood on the street, staring up at her third-floor balcony. I was horrified by the thought of Amie falling from there. She was on her balcony fighting for her life, and I'd been at home, less than a block away, enjoying Valentine's evening with my husband. I hadn't heard her screams, but I had listened to the police sirens in the early morning hours and wondered their cause.

I was working for NewsNation at that time, and they were interested in having me cover the story. Before I could get started, a few days after the murder, a detective rang my gate, asking if I had any Ring camera footage from the night of Amie's murder. I let him know that I was happy to help and that I had footage from that night. As the detective sat in my kitchen and downloaded the video from the computer, we talked about Amie, who was quite well-known in Hollywood circles. She'd dated several celebrities, including Dave Navarro, before she got engaged to comedian Drew Carey, host of *The Price Is Right*. The engagement only lasted eighteen months, but the two remained friends following their split. The homicide detective told me that he'd been going from house to house to obtain camera footage for hours, noting that police work wasn't nearly as glamorous as it was on television. I responded that neither was investigative journalism, and we laughed. Our jobs were more similar than people knew. The detective mentioned that he was looking for footage of Amie Harwick's accused killer, Gareth Pursehouse, before the murder. They'd already obtained video from other neighbors, showing Pursehouse parking hours before Amie's murder, but they were hoping my cameras might have captured something else. After obtaining the footage, the prosecution had successfully argued for the murder charge to include "lying in wait," and consequently, the court had revoked Pursehouse's bail.

The charge of murder while "lying in wait" is typically added to highlight the premeditation and deliberate planning that distinguishes this type of murder from other forms of homicide. In Los Angeles, a charge of lying in wait can be a special circumstance that can lead to enhanced penalties, including life imprisonment without parole or the death penalty.

There was no doubt that most people found Amie Harwick to be a beautiful woman, with her curvaceous figure, thick black hair, dark eyes, and porcelain-like skin. She often used black liner on her large eyes and wore red lipstick, which only enhanced her sexy allure. She'd been photographed quite a bit (once nude for *Playboy*), attending rock concerts in thigh-high boots and at speaking events, wearing crisp white blouses with pencil skirts that hugged her hips. Her friends adored her, happily sharing their stories about her kindness, her sense of adventure, and her beautiful soul with me. Although she'd had a great deal of success in her short life, Amie remained a loving, down-to-earth person who had an easy relationship with her own celebrity.

She had worked as a marriage and family therapist before earning a doctorate in human sexuality. Her book, *The New Sex Bible for Women: The Complete Guide to Sexual Self-Awareness and Intimacy*, published in 2014, wasn't a bestseller, but it generated enough interest for her to appear regularly on television and podcasts and helped her to create her own YouTube channel where she talked about, among other things, sexuality and intimacy. She was also close with her parents, Penny and Tom, who lived in Pennsylvania, and her brother, Chris Harwick. She also had a close-knit circle of friends in Los Angeles, comprising individuals from diverse backgrounds. Before becoming a therapist,

Harwood had been a *Playboy* model, a dancer, and a fire-eater, among other pursuits.

Valentine's Day

The story of Harwood's death is a horrible one that was difficult to comprehend. On February 14, 2020, just a few weeks before COVID would shut down all of Los Angeles, Amie, thirty-eight, drove from her Hollywood Hills home to meet her friends Rebecca and Sarah Rollins to see Miss Tosh perform at a burlesque show at the Globe Theatre. The group left the Globe Theatre around 9:15 p.m. and headed to Rebecca's place and then went to the NoMad Hotel to have appetizers. Rebecca, Sarah, and Amie took a photo that night, where Amie is captured smiling on the left of the picture, her arm draped around Sarah, with Rebecca next to Sarah. The three women left the NoMad Hotel at around midnight, and Sarah took an Uber home. When Sarah checked her phone forty-five minutes later, she received a text message from Amie, which read, "Send me the pics on the green couch." That was the last communication ever between the two friends.[20]

Amie also texted Robert Coshland, a photographer and close friend, in the early hours of February 16, 2020. He sent his last text to her around 11:00 p.m. on Valentine's Day, and she responded at 1:01 a.m. The two had been texting about plans for an upcoming trip to Scotland, which they wanted to take together. Fifteen minutes following Amie's texts to Robert

---

20 The events leading up to the murder of Amie Harwick are based on my notes at trial as well as opening statements by the prosecution and the defense. https://www.youtube.com/watch?v=mfe4C0Cxfp0

and Sarah, police raced to her home after receiving a radio call about a woman screaming on Mound Street. When they arrived at Amie's home, they found her under her third-floor balcony, unconscious and dying.

The call had come from Amie's roommate, Michael Herman, who had been asleep in a downstairs bedroom. He would later tell authorities that he woke up twice. The first time was when he heard something like a glass plate shattering on the ground. He'd fallen back to sleep after hearing the sound of breaking glass, but four hours later, he was awakened again by Amie screaming. He'd gotten up from the couch, walked to the door of the bedroom, and listened. It was then that he heard more screams and then choking sounds. He told police that the sound of her screams became muffled, and that's when he heard the choking and coughing sounds, and then, it sounded as if two bodies had fallen to the floor.

He realized that there was an intruder in the house and tried to find his phone to call the police. He screamed upstairs to let the intruder know he was there, yelling, "Hey, motherfucker," thinking that it might scare whoever was up there away. As Amie's sporadic screams continued, he opted to run and get help. He ran around the back of the house to the front and tried to exit through the front gate, but it was locked. He then managed to scale a side wall and knock on a neighbor's door. When there was no answer, he tried another door before locating a stranger on the street with a cell phone and using it to call 911.

When police finally arrived at the crime scene, they found Amie underneath her third-floor balcony, battered, unconscious, and struggling to breathe. There was no sign of anyone except Herman, the roommate who had called the police. The police immediately questioned him about the events of that evening, trying to discern whether he'd possibly assaulted Amie. However, when searching the home, they found that someone had broken in through a glass window, leaving glass shards scattered on the floor. The evidence that a person had broken into the home made them believe that someone else, in addition to Herman, had been present during the assault. They also located a syringe filled with a yellowish-brown substance, which they would later discover to be a lethal dose of nicotine.[21]

In the bodycam police video, a member of the fire department, Patrick Turner, was captured standing over Amie Harwick, checking for a pulse. There was a pulse when he checked the victim. "What we have right now is a female who looks like she either fell or struggled and fell from a third story balcony. The roommate that's here says he heard her screaming and thought she was probably being attacked. But instead of going to check on her, he went out on the street, is what he's claiming. He called the police and that he found her with the officers. There is some blood on his shirt, though. He says he doesn't think anyone else is here. She's breathing right now, but she's hurt bad."[22]

In trying to assess Harwick's injuries, Turner cut off the victim's clothing to assess her condition. He observed during his examination that Harwick had an extensive deformity to her pelvic region—her hips and waist line, and disfigurement

---

21 Facts of what was found at the home by police are based on witness testimony at trial and Police Bodycam footage shown to the jury at the trial. https://www.youtube.com/watch?v=zo73xXv_vsQ

22 First responder, Patrick Turner, testified at trial about examining and treating Harwick at her home. The quote is from actual trial testimony and the summary of Harwick's injuries is based on notes that I took during the trial. https://www.youtube.com/watch?v=vMbYNrKHiaM

to her neck and collarbone area and extreme softness to her ribs and her stomach area. He concluded that she was critically injured.

The next morning, Robert woke up to find his phone had blown up overnight. There were calls and texts from Herman that Amie had been assaulted, as well as a message from the police. Robert called the police back, and they asked him to come down to the Hollywood station. At the station, detectives informed Robert that Amie had been injured and was in the hospital, and they asked if he had any idea who could have hurt her. Robert told them he knew of one person. He explained that Amie had told him that if anything happened to her or if she disappeared, he should know it was Gareth. Robert had never seen Gareth, so he couldn't offer the police a description. He also didn't know Gareth's last name, so he contacted another friend, who provided him with the boyfriend's last name: Pursehouse.

Robert informed the homicide detectives that Pursehouse had physically abused Amie during their relationship and that she'd gotten a restraining order against him. It had expired in 2020. After the break-in, she'd considered getting a second one but abandoned the idea because she didn't think anyone would believe her. There was no actual evidence at the time that the man who'd broken into her home was Pursehouse. The month before she died, Amie accidentally ran into Pursehouse at an adult industry awards show. Pursehouse had approached her, screaming about how she'd "ruined his life." She told Robert that she'd been terrified and worried about Pursehouse's unhinged behavior.

After Robert's interrogation by the detectives, they took him to the waiting room where Herman had been seated. Robert recalled that Herman just looked at him and kept repeating, "It was really bad."

A few minutes later, they were both escorted back into the interrogation room, where one detective said softly, "We have some bad news. Amie died four hours ago."

The police investigation moved quickly. They quickly located Pursehouse's residence in Playa del Rey, only thirty miles from Santa Monica, California. Playa del Rey is a pricey beachside community with a mix of contemporary condos and single-family homes. When the police arrived at the house, Pursehouse was exiting his garage, along with a woman, Angeli G., who was in the passenger seat. She'd come over for a date, and he'd volunteered to drive her home. The woman in the car would later testify at trial that she'd biked from Santa Monica Beach to Playa del Rey to visit Pursehouse, whom she'd started dating about three weeks ago. When they pulled out of his garage, police immediately surrounded the car. Police instructed Pursehouse to exit his vehicle and lie face down on the pavement with his arms above his head. He was handcuffed and placed in a police car. The woman with him was given similar instructions and put in another police car, where officers questioned her en route to the station. When police ascertained she had nothing to do with Amie's murder, she was released.

Pursehouse was arrested at his home on February 15, 2020, charged with murder and residential burglary, and was released on $1 million bond, but then rearrested on the additional charge of lying in wait and held without bail. Between the first and second arrests, detectives found video obtained from neighbors that proved Pursehouse parked and then illegally entered Amie's home hours before he killed her. He remained behind bars at the Los Angeles County Jail for three years before his murder trial began in August 2023.

CHAPTER ELEVEN

The Stalker Turned Murderer

When I started my investigation, the first thing I did was walk around the corner from my home on Vine Street to Mound and speak to Amie's neighbors about what they'd seen and heard the night of her murder. Mound is a beautiful, but narrow two-way street, with homes in a wide variety of styles. The street dead-ends into a small cul-de-sac, where a sign warns drivers to avoid hitting a nearby wall. Most of Amie's neighbors knew her casually but had never really talked to her. One neighbor informed me that the neighbor next to Amie's home had a Ring camera that captured the killer behind Amie's home and had already provided the police with footage. I knocked on a few more doors, but was unable to contact the neighbor who'd provide the police with the Ring camera footage.

Once back home, I called her close friend, Robert Coshman, who had already spoken to the media publicly about Amie. We had some mutual friends, and I figured he might be willing to share more about Amie and their friendship. When I called, he was very friendly, soft spoken but quite deliberate with his words. He explained that he was busy working but would call me later. He'd rented his home out for filming and had to be present to ensure that nothing was disturbed by the crew or actors.

When he returned my call the next day, we spoke at length about Amie, his love for her, and how much he missed her. We made plans to meet at the Sunset Tower and grab some lunch, so that we could discuss Amie and his attempts to change the stalking laws in California to help women like her. Robert was a warm, kind person with dark brown hair and eyes, and a thin, athletic build. When he began to tell me about his best friend, his face softened. He was very specific in his recitation of the events that led up to Amie's tragic murder, leaving no detail unsaid. Robert and Amie first became friends in 2012, shortly after she'd ended her relationship with Pursehouse. She never mentioned Pursehouse in the early years of their friendship, mentioning the relationship to Robert for the first time in 2014.

"She'd loved him in the beginning, but then he'd become very controlling and very abusive," Robert explained. "He'd change after a bad episode, and be sweet and do all these things, but then something would happen again. She got a restraining order after he beat her up and gave her a black eye. Another time when he'd hit her, Amie called the police, and he convinced them to arrest her. She spent a night in jail before the police realized that he'd been the aggressor."

Around the time the two broke up in 2012, she'd been in the process of applying to be a family counselor at a local prison. Things were going well with the process, but just before the final interview, she'd been rejected. She'd discovered at the time that Pursehouse had sent nude photos of her to her prospective employer, which he'd gotten from her computer. Prior to their breakup, he'd installed software to monitor her. He was able to hack into everything on the computer, including her email.

The photos he'd sent to the prison were from *Playboy*. Amie had been angry because a prospective employer had seen her nude photos, and he refused to hire her. She told Robert that the photos had nothing to do with her qualification to do the job. Amie realized that she wasn't alone in being punished for her willingness to pose nude or overtly show her sexuality. She noted that many women were scorned and rejected by society because others felt they were too sexual or too promiscuous. She knew that many were unable to find work because they'd posed nude or had been sex workers or had other jobs deemed unsuitable by society. She felt that she could help them and it motivated her to abandon her job working in the prison.

"She did a course correction because of the rejection by the prison," Robert explained, and "opting instead to get a doctorate in advanced human sexuality."

After the nude photos were sent, things with her ex-boyfriend escalated. After a trip with friends, she came home to find that someone had broken into her home. Robert remembered that she'd called him the next day, saying that an intruder had stolen her photo albums, turned several things upside down, and erased her entire hard drive on her computer. She was sure it was Pursehouse.

"All kinds of objects in her home had been turned upside down," Robert said. "It was very strange and pretty creepy. When I examined her computer, I found that the intruder had deleted all the files. I was worried for her, so I suggested she get a webcam and have cameras in every room. She also got a new phone, computer, and new locks for the house. But Amie remained concerned, worrying that Pursehouse knew how to pick locks and that he was still watching her."

On January 16, 2020, Amie ran into Pursehouse.

"But only a month before her death," Robert said, "Amie attended an awards show and ran into him there. She called the next day and told me what happened. She didn't know he was going to be there, and when she saw him, she just stood there hoping he wouldn't recognize her. He was working as a photographer, and she was busy working the red-carpet event when he spotted her. She told me that he came running over to her, screaming at the top of his lungs, 'You ruined my life, you bitch.' He then fell to the ground, curled up in a ball, and began sobbing. He was reciting texts from eight years ago, and she became very concerned."

Robert recalled her saying how she went into counselor mode, trying to deescalate the situation because he was so distraught.

"She told him that it had been eight years, and she wanted him to meet other people because they couldn't be together. She always wanted to help everyone. She explained that he needed to live his life and she needed to live hers. She was kind, firm, and tried to let him down."

After the incident with Pursehouse, Amie was very shaken. Robert suggested she get a gun, but she opted instead for pepper spray. He also suggested that she try for another restraining order, but she felt there wasn't enough evidence, because all he'd really done was roll on the floor and cry. But Amie was clearly convinced that she was in danger. She wrote an email to herself the next day, detailing what had happened at the awards show with Pursehouse, how he'd behaved, and that he'd frightened her.

Pursehouse didn't find the email until months after her death. Amie emailed it to herself at 3:00 a.m., January 17, 2020, mere hours after she'd returned home from running into Pursehouse. The prosecutor would later read the email in court:

"Tonight I felt very scared. I went to the awards show with Hernando," Amie wrote. "When we arrived, I saw Gareth walk by with a camera; clearly, he was working. I decided to ignore him and just not look in that direction. I thought maybe he would not notice me.

"Hernando went to the bar to get a drink, and I was waiting with his friend in line. Gareth came up behind me and started screaming, 'why are you here? why are you here?' He looked dysregulated, and his eyes looked out of control. He started screaming you don't even like porn, you shouldn't be here, why are you here, and then he started looking like he was going to cry and was breathing heavily and flailing his arms around. I didn't want to scare anybody else, so I said, Hey, do you need to talk and we walked over to the side.

"We sat close by the bathrooms, I made sure to look, and made sure there were both security people and a lot of attendees very close by. He was sobbing, his head was in his hands, he was hyperventilating, he was distorting his face up, and shaking violently. I was scared and felt like I needed to neutralize the situation. I didn't think he was going to attack me in that moment, but this clearly showed me how obsessed he was. He told me that he thinks about me every day, and every day he cries. He told me that he lost his job when we broke up because he couldn't work. He told me that no matter what he did, he couldn't stop obsessing over me. He told me that I was a cheater and a liar, because he thought we were still together when I believed that we were broken up. He recited text messages that I had sent from this time frame, about nine years ago. He recalled the date, who they were too and exactly what was said, word for word. I couldn't believe it. I was very scared. He said he wasn't able to move on but he's dated, but nobody with me. He said he thinks about me constantly, and he can't watch together. Here are the songs that we liked, by the names that we called each other, or even smell vanilla or he has a panic attack. I sat with him for about twenty minutes or so, in my mind I wanted to neutralize the situation. I thought maybe in my mind that if I could make him see me as a neutral person, maybe these things would stop."[23]

Finally, she wrote that she was nervous about being more on her radar now, given the interaction. She wrote that she was terrified that he was obsessed with her for nine years, thinks about her every day, and can't move on, cries, and throws tantrums in this way.

Amie's fear was warranted, as, following their run-in at the awards show, Pursehouse found out where she lived and sent flowers to her home. He also texted her, but she quickly blocked him, and the communication stopped. Amie began to relax, putting the entire incident out of her head. Robert's concern also faded, as he had no idea that Pursehouse continued to stalk Amie, despite being blocked.

On the morning of Valentine's Day, Amie had breakfast with a friend. Robert called her at around 1:00 p.m. They both wished each other a happy Valentine's Day, said they loved each other, and that was the last time they ever spoke.

---

[23] Email sent by Amie Harwick to herself after encounter with Robert Pursehouse on the red carpet in January 17, 2020. Email was read aloud in court by Deputy District Attorney, Catherine Mariano.

"At least the last thing I said to her was that I loved her," Robert told me. "I first heard that something happened when I woke up the next morning. It was a Sunday. I looked at my phone and there were a whole bunch of text messages from Mike Herman, Amie's roommate, and several missed calls, including some from the police."

After the police had informed him that Amie had died, Robert tried to focus on what needed to be done. He recalled feeling shocked, but he started calling Amie's friends to tell them what had happened. The police asked him to refrain from calling Amie's parents; they'd been trying to have local law enforcement in Pennsylvania tell them in person. When he got in his car, he phoned Amie's friend, Marcy, who'd given him the ex-boyfriend's last name and who'd known Amie even longer than he. She'd been around in 2010 when Amie started dating Pursehouse. Marcy told Robert that Pursehouse had killed Amie; he'd never gotten over losing her.

Robert then called comedian Drew Carey, Amie's ex-fiancé, and told him that Amie had been killed.

Carey immediately said, "Oh, it's gotta be that guy," speaking of her stalker ex, Gareth Pursehouse. Carey struggled to understand that someone as loving and accepting as Amie had been killed in such a violent way. Although the comedian and the therapist had split in late 2018, Carey still loved her, and unbeknownst to Robert, the two had spoken recently about reconnecting. Carey put out a statement stating that Amie was "a beautiful person who didn't deserve to die like she did." Carey also publicly shared a petition calling for updated domestic violence laws.

After speaking with me, Robert agreed to send me a video of Amie's last birthday, which I used for a story we did about the murder on News Nation. He was also kind enough to introduce me to some of Amie's loving friends, a menagerie of fascinating women from all walks of life. I spoke to some of her friends, who would ultimately testify at the trial, and they told me about how much they missed Amie and how she'd helped them in so many ways. The more I learned about this young woman, the more I began to understand the enormity of loss for her friends and family.

Although all my initial information about the case came from Robert and other friends of Amie's, I tried calling many of Pursehouse's friends and family to get their perspective on his relationships with his family, friends and other women in his life. His family failed to return any of my calls, and most of his friends declined to be interviewed, citing concerns for their own safety. Pursehouse had become a national pariah, and most of the public was convinced of his guilt years before the case went to trial. When someone finally agreed to speak with me about the case, our conversation was relatively brief. He recalled that after his breakup with Amie, Pursehouse was depressed and unable to function. However, after some time had passed, he said that Pursehouse began dating and working again and seemed to have moved on with his life. He was shocked to see Pursehouse had been arrested for Amie's murder, claiming that he had seen nothing to suggest that Pursehouse was obsessed or about to kill anyone.

Rudy Torres, who was friends with both Pursehouse and Amie when they were together, had a very different experience. He recalled that after Amie left Pursehouse in 2012, he refused to accept that the relationship had ended. Torres claimed that Pursehouse was constantly contacting Amie and would not take no for an answer. Even as Amie tried to move on, Pursehouse refused to let her. When Torres told Pursehouse that it was time to move on and to leave Amie alone, Pursehouse stopped speaking to him.

Grace Stanley, a friend of Amie's for more than fourteen years, agreed with Torres's perceptions about Pursehouse. Amie phoned her after running into Pursehouse at the awards show. The two women spoke for a while about what had happened, with Amie saying that she'd been avoiding him for a long time because she was worried that he'd hurt her. She also texted Grace after getting a message from Pursehouse. Her text said, "I blocked him through text message, but because of his level of obsession, I definitely don't think I'm in the clear. I bought pepper spray at the house. My roommate is on alert, and I'm upping my security cameras." Sadly, there was nothing that Amie Harwick could do to forestall the inevitable. She tried and she failed to save her own life.

CHAPTER TWELVE

The Jury Hears the Case

Amie Harwick's trial began on August 29, 2023, with Deputy District Attorney Victor Avila giving the state's opening statement. The courtroom was filled with Amie's family and friends, who represented a diverse group of men and women from her very unique life. The women sported a rainbow of hair colors, ranging from black to pink, while their attire was just as varied. I spoke to one friend before court, who sat expertly applying her makeup while she chatted about Amie. She'd met Amie on a job, and the two had become close friends. Her friends were sex workers, trans activists, artists, musicians, and actors. Her parents and brother stood outside the court, warmly greeting the gathered crowd and graciously accepting their love and support. Pursehouse's family, in contrast, entered the courtroom quietly, taking their seats behind the defense table, taking pains to avoid looking at anyone. Pursehouse glanced up, looking very different from the rugged face captured in his mugshot, taken shortly after he allegedly murdered Amie. This man was heavier, his face puffy and pale, and his expression unreadable.

Prosecutor Avila began his opening statement by telling the jury that the defendant's actions on the day of Amie Harwick's murder were not impulsive but were rather a deliberate plan to end her life. He drove to Harwick's home, Avila stated, with a deliberate plan to murder Amie Harwick, waiting in her home for several hours. He claimed that the evidence presented by the state would show that Gareth Pursehouse murdered Amie Harwick because he was obsessed with her. When she rejected his advances and cut off all contact, the defendant resolved to punish her. He broke into her house with a syringe loaded with a lethal dose of nicotine; he waited hours for her to come home. After arriving home, she went to her third-story bedroom, and Pursehouse deliberately attacked her.

I sat in the back row, typing furiously as Avila set out the events that he alleged led to Harwick's murder, occasionally glancing over at Pursehouse, who showed no emotion, except to occasionally glance up at the ceiling.

"Let's get right into it," Avila remarked, glancing down at his notes. He went through Amie and Pursehouse's history, noting that they'd dated ten years ago and were together for around eighteen months. Harwick obtained a restraining order against the defendant, effectively ending the relationship, and moved on with her life. In 2020, she accompanied her friend, Dr. Hernando Chavez, a fellow therapist, to a ZBIZ awards show. They both worked in the adult film industry, helping people in that industry who needed therapy and, as such, were invited to an adult film awards show. Chavez and Harwick arrived together at the Marriott hotel that evening.[24]

"She was excited to be there," Avila said. "However, that all changed when the defendant arrived. The defendant is actually a computer programmer, but one of his side jobs is photography, and he'd been hired to photograph folks on the red carpet."

Avila directed his attention to the jury.

"Fernando Chavez will tell you that he went to get drinks for a moment, and he was called back because a commotion happened. He got back there to see that the defendant was crying and upset."

Avila claimed that after seeing Pursehouse, Amie's demeanor changed. She "was putting on a face now," taking photographs on the red carpet. She was stoic. As the awards ceremony was about to end, the defendant approached her again and asked to talk. She agreed and she went with him to try to calm the situation down. Within forty-five minutes, the conversation ended, and she left, going to the parking lot. She was supposed to go to another show, but she canceled to go to a restaurant to talk to Chavez. She told Chavez that she was going to increase security at her home. He offered to drive her home, but she declined.

When she arrived home, she wrote an email that night and sent it to herself. The email demonstrated Amie's state of mind: she feared for her safety and wanted to create a record in case something happened to her. The end of her email was sadly prescient.

---

[24] The quotes from the opening statement of Prosecutor Avila are based on my courtroom notes as well as upon video of the trial that I reviewed online at https://www.youtube.com/watch?v=mfe4C0C

"At the end of the conversation, I told him my friend Hernando was waiting for me," she wrote. "I asked him how he would like to end this conversation. I told him that we didn't have to be brutal enemies. I told him that we will not be friends and we will not be talking, but that we don't have to be enemies and told him I was sorry for anything I did that was hurtful all of those years ago, and I told him that I forgave him. He asked for a hug, and I told him that was not a good idea, and he started to cry. Eventually, he walked away."

As Amie had feared, the very next day, Pursehouse texted her that he'd found her number. He engaged in text messages with her and wanted to talk with her and meet with her. She tried to tell him that there was no future for them, without setting him off again.

"I am sure that there is a lot more that you want to process and say to me. I think that was a lot for both of us. I hope you were able to hear me last night when I said I was sorry for anything that caused you suffering and that I forgave you for the things you did to me. I think it's best to have some space right now, and I don't mean that in a negative way. The past is sad, and truly, for both of us. I think we ended our talk last night well. We can be civil with distance, respect each other, and move forward with our lives."

Pursehouse's reply was tinged with hostility and regret. "So, you are still just gone, which is exactly my nightmare, and sadly what I expect."

After the exchange, Harwick texted her friend, Hernando Chavez, letting him know that Pursehouse had located her cell number and texted, but she'd set a boundary with him, telling him things were finished. Again, Pursehouse refused to acknowledge reality and continued to text her that night, refusing to accept the situation as it was. Harwick didn't respond and blocked his number; she also installed new locks on her home and added security cameras to the middle floor. In an effort to protect herself, she installed two Ring cameras to capture the vacant lot behind the home.

The prosecutor played the jury the Ring camera footage from behind the neighbor's home, which captured the defendant on the night of Harwick's murder, at 8:53 p.m., approaching the cameras before pulling the first one down and repeating the same action with the second camera. Amie was with her friends at the time, unaware that Pursehouse was in her home, waiting for her. Avila took the jury through Amie's arrival home at around 1:00 a.m. He stated that, although no video captured what happened to Harwick inside the house, there was evidence indicating that an altercation had occurred. Amie's necklace from that night was broken, and in the corner of the third-floor media room, her jacket was there, along with a puddle of urine. Her body showed that she'd been in a fight for her life. Her fingernails were later swabbed and tested, and the DNA matched that of Gareth Pursehouse.

The jury was then played a chilling excerpt of the 911 call made by Amie's roommate, Mike Herman, who had successfully escaped the home and phoned 911, nine minutes after Harwick's first text.

Herman told the operator, "I heard her screaming. I know she was being attacked. I heard her being thrown to the ground."

I glanced over at Pursehouse at that moment, and he was looking down, completely expressionless, seemingly unmoved by the hysteria in Herman's voice. Prosecutor Avila gave the jurors a short timeline of the last moments of Harwick's life.

"Harwick was in a debilitated state after being strangled, and when her roommate yelled up the stairs, the defendant panicked. He opened the door to the balcony, took her to the balcony, and threw her body over the three-story balcony. Blood that was on his hands after hitting Harwick transferred to the door that led to the balcony."

When police searched the home, they also found a syringe filled with a yellow liquid. The cause of death, which the coroner would testify to, was severe trauma from that fall, including damage to the brain, the liver, the pelvis, and manual strangulation. As Amie's body lay there on the concrete, the kitchen door remained open, so that Pursehouse could leave and go back the same way he'd come. His exit was captured by the Ring cameras behind Amie's neighbor's house.

Officers initially thought that the liquid in the syringe was heroin, but when the syringe was sent to LAPD labs, they couldn't identify the contents. Ultimately, the liquid from the syringe was sent to the FBI for a more comprehensive test, and they determined it was nicotine. An expert would later testify that that amount of nicotine in that pure form, if injected into Amy Harwick, would have killed her. Additionally, that particular poison was not readily detectable in the body.

I spotted Robert Coshland standing in the hallway outside the courtroom, and we chatted about his thoughts regarding the opening statement. He thought that Avila had done a good job, but it was very hard for him to hear about Amie's fear and the last moments of her life. After a few minutes, I asked if he would be comfortable introducing me to Amie's parents. He was close with them and had lent them a great deal of support in the years following Amie's murder. He'd also been in close contact with them prior to the trial, spending a great deal of time with them and helping them to navigate trips to the courthouse. After Robert made the introductions, he stepped away to speak with someone. Tom and Penny Harwick weren't really in the mood to talk, but they understood that I was sympathetic and knew that I was a neighbor of Amie's. Though they were still struggling with Amie's loss, their focus was on making sure that Pursehouse was convicted. Mrs. Harwick said that it's been very difficult to be in Los Angeles for such a long time, but it was something that they had to do. When I asked if she'd be open to doing an interview with NewsNation to talk about Amie, she said not right now, but said that Amie's brother, Chris, would likely be willing to speak with me. Before leaving Robert to chat with them, I expressed my sorrow about Amie's passing and added that she was clearly a very special person, and that all the people I'd interviewed missed her terribly.

It was always hard to talk to close relatives of victims, especially at a trial. After our conversation, a part of me felt uncomfortable about bothering Amie's parents after they'd just heard the details of their daughter's murder. But I knew that even during the darkest parts of a trial, the victim's relatives were generally invested in making sure that their loved one's life was not forgotten in the midst of the proceedings. Coverage of trials often focuses primarily on the defendant and the witnesses, with the victim's life becoming a footnote.

The defense's opening statement began after the fifteen-minute break. Attorney Joseph Miskovice read from Pursehouse's text to Amie after unexpectedly running into her, after not having seen her for eight years.[25]

"I have so much I need to say. Please give me a chance to say it. So, I could have just said it. Please. Please. Can we meet again? It feels the same as when I wrote you that long list of what I would miss about you, and heard nothing back. Just reaching out into the darkness, trying to stop falling. I wish I could do something more. But reaching out to you is a crippling action that I'd actually contemplated over the past few months, just to say to you the word help. Admitting to you how hurt I am is so embarrassing and painful, which demolishes me even more. Please don't vanish on me. Please don't let me go through that again. Please call me."

Miskovice argued to the jury that the evidence would show that the chance meeting between Harwick and Pursehouse sent him into a debilitating depression that he was not able to overcome. He was begging her for help and pleading with her for a chance to talk to her. The evidence, he argued, would show that running into her at the event sent him into a deep fog of depression and made him think that the only way to get relief from that pain was to go and talk to her. The attorney stated that the ultimate question for the jury was what Pursehouse intended to do when he broke into Amie's house in 2020, claiming that the evidence would show that his only intention was to speak to her that night and that he never intended to kill her.

[25] Texts from Defendant Gareth Pursehouse after seeing Amie Harwick for the first time in eight years are based on my trial notes as well as video of Defense Attorney Miskovice opening statement. https://www.youtube.com/watch?v=mfe4C0Cxfp0

The Defense

The defense began their effort to prove to the jury that the only reason Pursehouse went to Harwick's house on the evening of February 14 was to talk to her. He never intended to kill her. The importance of the argument for Pursehouse was that if the defense could prove that Pursehouse didn't intend to kill, the jury could potentially acquit him on the first-degree murder charge. It was a steep hill for the defense to climb, but they did their best in the opening statement to paint Pursehouse as a crushed and broken man who simply believed that if he could speak with Harwick, he would be able to move on with his life.

Miskovice worked to establish that Pursehouse told Harwick repeatedly that he simply wanted to talk. He argued that after Pursehouse saw Harwick at the awards show, he literally lost control of his emotions and was plunged once again into the pain he'd experienced following his breakup with Harwick years ago. However, he realized that when Amie agreed to speak to him on the red carpet, he was able to stand up and regain his composure. Later that night, Pursehouse walked up to the table where Harwick was seated and whispered, "Can we talk again tonight?" Shortly thereafter, the two of them sat on a bench and talked again, but after forty-five minutes, Amie told Pursehouse that she had to go. The conversation was cut short, and Pursehouse asked if they could meet again, and Harwick replied that it wasn't a good idea.

I jotted down the comment, aware that the lawyer was not so subtly suggesting that if Harwick had allowed Pursehouse to discuss his feelings extensively, he likely would not have broken into her house in a desperate effort to continue the conversation.

It seemed like a stretch to me, but from what I'd seen of the evidence, the defense wasn't working with much.

On January 18, 2020, after sending text messages the day before, Pursehouse left a voice message for Harwick in which he begged her to give him a chance to talk to her again.

"Please," he can be heard saying between sobs.

"She didn't respond to his pleas for help," the lawyer added. "She blocks his number."

In the days after this encounter, a friend, Miss Minasaka, noticed that he was down and depressed, and she asked him if he was okay. He told her that he is "rarely okay." He described his state of mind as feeling like a chain was pulling down on him that he pretends doesn't exist but that cripples him in so many ways in life. Miss Minasaka was concerned that he might hurt himself and suggested things that he might do to alleviate his depression. The depth of depression that he was in was so acute that the only thing he thought he could do to get released from this depression was to speak with Amie.

Miskovice then told the jury that the defense would have an accident reconstruction expert testify as to how Harwick ended up on the concrete patio, twenty feet beneath the third-floor balcony. The expert was going to tell the jury how one can use mathematical equations to examine the parameters that determine where someone came to rest and identify the possible starting points that could have resulted in where Harwick's body was found. He had excluded several scenarios and identified two possible scenarios that explain how Harwick ended up on the payment below the balcony. One likely scenario was that Harwick fell after hanging off the balcony, gripping the balcony railing with either one or two feet, and using the awning to brace her weight, before falling from that position. He claimed that the jury would see photographs of damage to the awning that supported the expert's conclusions.

The defense then told the jury one likely scenario of how Amie Harwick "came to rest" on the patio under the third-floor balcony of her home.

"Miss Harwick comes home, encounters Mr. Pursehouse, screams, waking up Michael Herman, causing him to go to the stairs. He shouts up at them. Upon hearing him shouting up, a struggle ensues between Miss Harwick and Mr. Pursehouse. In a panic, she runs through her bedroom to her balcony, climbs up and over the railing, attempts to lower herself and climb down, and falls."

He admitted in his final remarks that Pursehouse broke into Harwick's home, and had he not been there, he would not have caused the chain of actions that led to her death but continued to claim that Pursehouse never intended to kill her. He asked the jury to find Pursehouse guilty of the appropriate charge, which was not murder.

While I appreciated the defense's effort to get the jury to consider a lesser charge, I found the rest of the opening statement to be weak and not terribly convincing. My thoughts were echoed in the jurors' faces as Miskovice spoke about how Amie had met her demise. They'd listened, but not in the same intent way that they'd listened to the prosecutor. They never revealed doubt or any obvious emotion, but their restrained, polite interest spoke volumes.

The Witnesses

Most of the prosecution's witnesses were fairly compelling in their testimony about Amie's state of mind after running into Pursehouse a month before her death. Amie had spoken to many of them about her fears regarding Pursehouse's texts and detailed her efforts to improve security around her home. When the detectives who'd investigated the murder took the stand, their observations from the scene of the crime were both disturbing and heartbreaking.

When Detective Masterson took the witness stand, I recognized him. I initially thought that Masterson was a friend of Amie's because of his long gray hair and relaxed demeanor. Despite his suit and tie, he didn't look anything like the other detectives milling around the courthouse, waiting to testify. When I asked Robert Coshland who he was, he explained that he was the homicide detective who investigated Amie's murder. He had since retired from the police force, which explained his long hair and friendly manner.

Masterson took the stand and testified about the evidence found in Harwick's home, as well as the DNA evidence that police collected. Masterson said that the police had an exterior log of evidence, which covered the outside of the house. The exterior crime scene log was started earlier, at 1:27 a.m., once the responding police determined that it was a homicide scene. The police also maintain a log, referred to as the interior crime scene, which is more restrictive because they want to keep that crime scene as pristine as possible. They started an interior crime scene log at 5:00 a.m.

The prosecution showed Detective Masterson photos of a statue and fence on the Harwick property. Masterson testified that the statue and the fence were outside of the house, and he'd asked other investigators on the scene to have the area swabbed for DNA to see if it would show someone had broken into the home. Masterson was asked to identify another photo that depicted the French doors, showing broken glass from the doors with a red stain, likely dried blood, on the wood. The stain was also swabbed for DNA.

Avila also put a photo of Amie's leather jacket, which was on the floor of the media room next to broken beads and a cross from the rosary necklace she'd worn that evening to the burlesque show. Several of her friends, seated in the courtroom, looked at their hands, distraught over seeing the remains of one of Amie's favorite necklaces. Masterson also testified about finding a puddle of urine near the necklace and jacket and said that it was swabbed for DNA as well, as was the syringe with nicotine that was found on the ground of the balcony, near the master bedroom.

Next was the testimony of Aspen Jamison, an adult film star, who'd also attended the adult film awards on the same night as Amie Harwick and Hernando Chavez. After walking the red carpet, Jamison spotted her friend, Dr. Hernando Chavez, waiting to go on the red carpet at around 7:30 p.m. He introduced her to Amie Harwick, a fellow sex therapist, and said that both were attending the show to network. After chatting for a minute, he noticed that Jamison was nervous and offered to get her a drink. He asked her to stay with Amie while he went and got everyone drinks. Jamison said that she engaged in small talk with Amie before they were approached by an angry Pursehouse, who said to Amie, "Funny seeing you here." He interrupted their conversation and failed to introduce himself to Jamison. She remained silent while Amie spoke to Pursehouse, and she heard some of their conversation, during which he called her a hypocrite and said he didn't know why she was there. He made it seem like she'd never approved of the adult film industry.

Jamison then texted and called Hernando Chavez during Amie's conversation with Pursehouse.

She testified, "I felt bad for her because she was in a very awkward position, and it felt like they'd just broken up, and it seemed like he was an ex-boyfriend, but it definitely felt fresh and new. It seemed like she needed help."

After hearing from Amie's friends about her tense encounter with an angry Pursehouse, the prosecution called a woman I'd seen sitting outside the courtroom for several days. She was alone, and it appeared that she didn't know Amie's parents or any of her friends. I finally approached her and said hello, hoping that she'd tell me her role in the trial. She refused to give her name and quietly admitted that she wasn't a friend of Amie's. Before I could inquire further about her role, someone approached and steered her away from me.

It turned out that the woman, Angel Gangel, had dated Pursehouse in the weeks before Amie's death. When she took the stand, she testified that she'd met Gareth on Tinder, only two or three weeks before Valentine's Day. She'd communicated with him for a bit before the two became intimate. She told the prosecutor that she'd had intimate relations with Pursehouse on two to four different occasions and expected to spend Valentine's night with him. When she didn't hear from him, she texted him during the day, asking, "What are you up to? And why haven't you asked me out tonight?" She punctuated the text with a sad face.

Pursehouse responded that evening, at 6:48 p.m., saying he was at home, and "I told you that I am busy all week." She told jurors that she found his response annoying, but there wasn't much she could do about it. He texted the next morning, writing, "Morning Sunshine. What are you up to?"[26]

"I just got back from walking the dogs. Think I'm going to ride my bike to the beach. It's gorgeous out. Oh, and getting quotes for a trip."

Angel was planning a vacation and assessing prices. The two discussed whether they wanted to hang out and then what to do.

Angel recalled that "he suggested maybe going to the shooting range, but I wanted to go to the beach because it was a beautiful day. He said he couldn't go in the sun because his skin was sensitive, so he couldn't be outside." She agreed to a jump on her bike and come over to hang out with Pursehouse.

Her ride from Santa Monica Beach to Playa del Rey, where he lived, took more than an hour.

"I got a jump bike electronic bike. I arrived at his house at 1:40 p.m. I left my house at 12:29 p.m."

At around 1:40 p.m., Gareth greeted her, and she testified that they "went out to his place and he was doing some work on the French doors at the front of his place and I helped him organize his apartment." She was there for around two hours.

When asked by the prosecutor about his mood when she arrived, she stated, "He greeted me and after that, he seemed sad and distant." She noted that they were not intimate that day, but they'd hugged and may have kissed.

---

[26] The quotation is based on my trial notes as well as video of Angel's trial testimony in court. https://www.youtube.com/watch?v=PaO19DkV-hs&t=36s

When asked about his appearance that day, Angel replied, "There was a bruise under his eye and maybe some scratches on his face. I think it was his right eye. He had a bruise. It looked like a small black eye." When asked by the prosecutor to give more details on the scratches and their location, she added, "There were a couple on his neck and face, if I remember correctly. I want to say the right side of his face. Maybe three or four scratches. They were red and maybe a half inch [long]."

She asked Pursehouse how he'd gotten the bruise, and he claimed to have cut himself shaving. She also recalled that the condition of his apartment that day bothered her.

"It was disorganized. I think he was doing construction work on his front patio doors, and all his things were piled away from that area. And it was messy."

Prosecutors then asked if Pursehouse had ever mentioned Amie Harwick or having gone through a bad breakup; she said no. During cross-examination, she was compelled to retract that answer because she'd previously claimed to detectives that he had an excruciating breakup with an ex-girlfriend.

One of Pursehouse's defense attorneys, Robin Bernstein-Lev, asked if Angel spent much time talking to Pursehouse.

She replied, "We didn't chat much, and he was kind of staring off into space, doing something electrical on the door." She told him that she truly felt sorry for him and wanted to be there when he was sad, in the same way he felt sad.

Following their afternoon together, Pursehouse offered to drive her home. She opted to leave the bike behind, and they walked out the back of his residence and got into his car, which was in a detached garage. They were immediately blocked in by police cars, and officers brandishing weapons and telling

Pursehouse to exit the car. Angel recalled that Pursehouse's only comment to her before getting out of the car was, "Just do what they say." After Pursehouse was placed in a police car and driven away, she was detained and questioned by the police and ultimately driven to the impound lot to retrieve her purse from Pursehouse's car.

The Closing

The closing statements in the Harwick trial were as disturbing, with the prosecution going to great lengths to convince the jury that the evidence showed Pursehouse meticulously planned to murder Harwick and then successfully executed his plan, hurling Harwick off the balcony and leaving her to die on the pavement below.

"Time to hold the defendant accountable for his actions," Deputy District Attorney Avila said coldly. "There is only one reasonable interpretation that points to his guilt: burglary, murder, and lying in wait." He said that whatever love Pursehouse had was in the past; that love has turned to anger and hate. He deliberately chose Valentine's Day to end her life. He wanted to make a statement, and he wanted his face to be the last one that Amie Harwick ever saw, purposely not wearing a mask in those final moments of her life.

Avila, his tone a mix of defiance and anger, shared his final thoughts with the jury about Pursehouse and why he truly killed Amie Harwick.

"If Amie lives, his life is over. She will identify him and report the incident to the police. He is done," Avila said, his voice tinged with anger. "He is selfish and only cares about himself and his pain. I am not asking to vote guilty for feeling sympathy for Amie Harwick. Don't let that enter into your deliberations. Do not factor in punishment, bias, passion, speculation, or other evidence that you have never heard. There is no talking, there is no discussion; she gets surprised, she gets scared, he attacks her. When he lifts her over the balcony, he knows how high it is (twenty-one feet). He plans on finishing her off; she won't be able to identify him if she is dead."

Pursehouse's lawyer, Robin Bernstein-Lev, gave the closing statement for the defense. She began by addressing why Pursehouse broke into Amie Harwick's house, once again telling the jury that he went there because he was desperate to talk to her.

"You heard a lot of evidence, you had the chance to see the email Amie had to herself describing the encounter and had an opportunity to hear from witnesses whom Amie spoke to about it. You also had the opportunity to see Gareth's texts to Amie Harwick—all this paints a picture of the pain that Pursehouse experienced after the breakup back in 2012. He struggled in all those intervening years to deal with the daily pain that was described to her in those text messages. He tried to control that struggle, making an effort to regain his equilibrium. He dated other women, had a successful career, and had a good life. But he was unable to replicate the deep intimacy that he'd forged with Harwick with anyone else. This was a man in crisis."

Again, I looked at Pursehouse; his expression remained stoic, his eyes cast down. He didn't even seem to be listening as his lawyer spoke about his difficult past. His lack of expression was odd, given that we'd seen and heard about his sensitivity, pain, and tears throughout the trial. But as his lawyer attempted once again to convince the jury of Pursehouse's uncontrollable emotions, he seemingly remained contained and distant from the proceedings. It was possible that he was on medication that had not only caused his almost catatonic state but also his extreme weight gain.

Bernstein-Lev then attempted to undercut the importance to the jury of the emails that Harwick had sent to herself and to friends about her fear of Pursehouse.

"You cannot use this evidence in any way to decide whether or not he intended her harm. All of her statements about her fear are not something you can consider when thinking about Pursehouse's state of mind or his intentions."

The lawyer went on to argue that while the prosecution claimed that Pursehouse acted out of anger when he arrived at Amie Harwick's home, he had intended to kill and murder her.

"But where is the anger in those messages?" she asked the jury. "He is supplicant to her. He's not aggressive. He's not entitled. He's just telling her he's vulnerable. If he was angry at her for being blocked, why wouldn't that anger have surfaced all those years ago when they first broke up? Why wait all those years? Anger was not his motivation; it would have surfaced way earlier."

She argued that the prosecution had provided no evidence that Harwick didn't go out onto the balcony on her own volition and try to climb over the balcony to escape, noting that jurors had seen an earlier photo of her in which she posed while perched on the balcony. She was comfortable with being on the balcony and likely tried to use the railing to get down from the third floor, falling in her attempt.

Bernstein-Lev also attacked Hernando Chavez's testimony regarding Pursehouse's comments to Amie at the adult film awards. She argued that the prosecution provided some very unreliable evidence at trial, noting that Chavez told the jury that Pursehouse yelled at Harwick that she'd "fuckin' ruined" his life.

"'You fuckin' ruined my life'"—'fuckin'' is something that he says in his regular vocabulary, but doesn't mean he is hostile or angry," the lawyer continued. "Chavez admitted that he actually didn't hear him call her a bitch, that was a new recollection. Disregard Chavez's statement that GP called Amie Harwick a bitch; she didn't even note it in her email."

The defense also argued that despite the prosecution's claim, Pursehouse had not punched Harwick in the face.

"If she'd been punched in the face, there would have been blood. But there is no blood on the balcony, bedroom, or anywhere to substantiate a claim that she was punched in the face. All blood is where she landed."

Finally, the defense argued that the prosecution had a theory that Pursehouse intended to use the nicotine syringe as a weapon, arguing that there were problems with that theory. The nicotine was old and dated; the color would take years to break down, meaning that Pursehouse had not acquired the poison to hurt Amie Harwick.

"Her death was never his goal," Bernstein-Lev said. "It was not to be used on Amie Harwick" and "not intended to be a weapon." She added that after his arrest, Pursehouse was put on suicide watch, insinuating that he'd brought the syringe to kill himself.

The jury found Gareth Pursehouse guilty of first-degree murder in the death of Hollywood therapist Amie Harwick, with the special circumstance of lying in wait and first-degree burglary. Before Pursehouse's sentencing, her mother, Penny Harwick, took the stand to give her impact statement. Although I'd heard many family members make victim statements before, Penny Harwick's remarks about her daughter moved me to tears. I can still remember most of what she said that day about her beloved daughter. Below is just a small part of what Penny read to the courtroom about her extraordinary child, Amie Harwick.

"There is a song in the musical *Rent* that's called '525,600 minutes: How Do You Measure a Year in a Life.' It's times four now, because she has been taken from us almost four years ago. Do you measure her life through credentials? Undergraduate studies from California Polytechnic State University? Through her master of arts in clinical psychology from Pepperdine? Her doctorate in human sexuality from the Institute of the Advanced Study of Human Sexuality? Do you measure it through love of music, Tori Amos, Depeche Mode, Christina Perry, heavy metal, through accomplishments? She was a model, a therapist, an author, a personal trainer, she released an exercise video, she created podcasts, she wrote magazine articles, she was a fire eater, a dancer, a budding photographer, a bartender. Do we measure her life through what's missing? A thousand or so phone calls that haven't come? Empty chairs at family tables? Through her visits home and our visits to LA? Do we measure it by her relationships? She was a daughter, a sister, a granddaughter, an aunt, a wife, a stepmom, a niece, and a friend.

"I want to talk about hands and touch. Your hands were filled with hatred and vitriol. Your hands were focused on hurting Amie and causing pain. Your touch was to punish Amie for rejecting you. We all know what your hands accomplished. But I want you to know that your touch was not the last touch that Amie felt or remembered. Helping hands arrived after you ran away. Hands trained to offer aid and assistance.... Amie felt those interventions, and she felt their touch. She never regained consciousness, but I am positive she knew that people were trying to help her. They could not undo the harm you inflicted.

"Don't worry, Amie, you didn't simply visit this world. Your light will shine forever. You said that Amie ruined your life, Gareth Pursehouse. But that's not true; you managed to do that all by yourself. What is true is that you fractured my life; part of me is buried with my daughter. I fight each and every day to be present for the rest of my family, to engage in life, and to try and heal that fracture. Every day is a battle that I am determined to win."

On December 6, 2023, Pursehouse was sentenced to life in prison without the possibility of parole. Following the sentencing, I called Harwick's good friend, Robert Coshland, to get his reaction. He was relieved that Pursehouse had been found guilty, but he noted that there still is no closure for him or her family. After hearing all the testimony at the trial, Robert confided to me that it was still hard to believe that Pursehouse had gone to Harwick's house with the intention of killing her.

Coshland noted that the best way he could see to deal with Harwick's murder was to continue to focus on raising funds for a memorial to Amie Harwick, which he told me would be located at the Hollywood Forever Cemetery, a Hollywood landmark where many famous departed celebrities now reside. As he'd told me when we first met, he and many of Harwick's friends began raising funds for a statue to memorialize Harwick along with beloved cat, Marquis de Chat. They created a website to raise funds for the statue delineating the purpose was to "celebrate

Amie's work as a therapist, author, and champion of women. The memorial will be classical in nature and will be imbued with the symbolism of the goddess Aphrodite."[27]

[27] "Donate to the Dr. Amie Harwick Memorial Statue, Organized by Robert Coshland." Gofundme.com, www.gofundme.com/f/the-dr-amie-harwick-memorial-statue. Accessed 13 Nov. 2025.

ACKNOWLEDGMENTS

Writing this book was the fulfillment of a dream for me that started when I was quite young. I spent many days lingering in bookstores with my parents and my three siblings, hoping that one day I would have a book on the shelves that people would want to read. It was a long journey to *Murder and The Media: Behind the Scenes of Four High Profile Murders.* I never would have finished the journey without the love and support of my husband, Jody Zucker, who has been there for all the prison visits, the late night calls from inmates, and the long drives across various states to interview victims, lawyers, murderers, judges, and investigators. I am also grateful to my agent and my friend, Scott Kaufman, who always was there to answer my calls and to calm me down. I also need to thank my diligent and very talented editors,Caitlin Burdette and Debra Englander, at Post Hill Press who helped me navigate the difficult path to publication.

ABOUT THE AUTHOR

Allison Weiner is an Emmy Award–winning producer who has worked with many of the top journalists in the country, including Diane Sawyer, Christopher Cuomo, Elizabeth Vargas, Dan Abrams, Ashley Banfield, John Quinones, and many others. She has appeared on News Nation, CNN, ABC News 20/20, HLN, Inside Edition, Entertainment Tonight, Extra, Access Hollywood, and many other networks reporting on high-profile crime stories. She was an entertainment industry litigator before she became a journalist. A graduate of Columbia University and the University of Southern California Law, she practiced law and then segued to journalism, writing for *Los Angeles Magazine*, *Entertainment Weekly*, *Vanity Fair*, and *Buzz*. She covered law and the industry at *Entertainment Weekly*, getting exclusives with James Gandolfini during his contract dispute, Paul Reubens, and with the three teens convicted for killing a young girl after listening to songs by the band Slayer. While at *Entertainment Weekly*, Weiner covered the trials of Winona Ryder, Robert Blake, Michael Jackson, and others. She then worked for *The New York Times*, writing a profile of the legendary Hollywood lawyer Bert Fields, a person of interest in the FBI's investigation of Anthony Pellicano, celebrity private eye. She wrote exclusive pieces about the federal investigation exploring Pellicano's connection to many Los Angeles power brokers including Brad Grey, Ron Burkle, and Ron Meyer. After refusing to name her sources on the Pellicano piece, the FBI opened an investigation to determine her sources on the story. While at *The New York Times*, Weiner also wrote about the criminal investigation into the tactics of local LA paparazzi and attempts by the DA to bring conspiracy charges against the photographers.

After working for *The New York Times*, Weiner wrote crime-related stories for *The Huffington Post, Deadline Hollywood, The Daily Beast, Newsweek, The Hollywood Reporter, The Los Angeles Times*, and many others. She worked as a producer for ABC's 20/20 for six years, recently winning an Emmy award for work on the Diane Sawyer special, "Escape from a House of Horrors."

Ms. Weiner currently works as a senior investigative producer on staff at News Nation.